The Hecht Prize Anthology

2005-2009

The Hecht Prize Anthology

2005-2009

edited by

Joseph Harrison

WAYWISER

First published in 2011 by

THE WAYWISER PRESS

Bench House, 82 London Road, Chipping Norton, Oxfordshire OX7 5FN, UK
P.O. Box 6205, Baltimore, MD 21206, USA
http://waywiser-press.com

Editor-in-Chief
Philip Hoy

Senior American Editor
Joseph Harrison

Associate Editors
Eric McHenry   Clive Watkins   Greg Williamson

This collection and introduction © Joseph Harrison, 2011

Copyright of poems featured in this anthology rests with authors and other
rights holders as cited in the acknowledgments section,
which constitutes an extension of this copyright page.

All rights reserved

A CIP catalogue record for this book is available from the British Library

ISBN 978-1-904130-46-8

Printed and bound by
T J International Ltd., Padstow, Cornwall, PL28 8RW

Contents

Editor's Introduction ... 17

CRAIG ARNOLD

Incubus ... 21

BRUCE BERGER

Transmigration ... 25
Confession ... 26

PETER BETHANIS

American Future ... 30
The Deer in the Barns ... 31

KIMBERLY BURWICK

Everything Lush I Know ... 32
These Nails, They Point Upwards ... 33
My Arrows Are Not Sharp ... 34
The Norway Tree ... 35
Must One Wait For It To Wither? ... 36

MICHAELA CARTER

The Debutante Ball ... 37
When We Speak of Love ... 38

KEN CHEN

My Father and My Mother Decide My Future and How
   Could We Forget Wang Wei?   39

SCOTT COFFEL

Light-Years from My Redemption   42
In the Throes of Advanced Study   43
Andrei and Natasha   44
Cockeyed Louie   45
The Emerald City   46
Hordes of Indigent Psychologists   47
Mild Worlds Elsewhere   48

ANDREW COX

Two Plus Two Equals Five   50
The American Museum   51

MORRI CREECH

World Enough   53
The Canto of Ulysses   55
For the Rebel Angels   57
The Resurrection of the Body   58
Listening to the Earth   61
Firstfruits   63

GREGORY CROSBY

from The Book of Erros
   I   65
   XVII   66

ERICA DAWSON

Nappyhead	68
Doll Baby	70
OCD	72
Credo	73
Parallax	74
Bees in the Attic	76

ANTHONY DEATON

After Troy	80
The Refusal	82
Homeward, Angel	84

MATT DONOVAN

Prelude for Musical Glasses	86
Exit Pursued by Bear	88
On the Wheel Constructed for the 400th Anniversary of Columbus in the New World	90

MOLLY FISK

Prayer for Joe's Taco Lounge, Mill Valley	93
Rowing, November	94
Pantoum Without Hope of Rescue	95

MARTHA GREENWALD

The Last Secretary	97
Other Prohibited Items	98

DANIEL GROVES

A Dog's Life	100
Portrait	101
Novella	103
Balder –	105
A Stranger Here	107

JAMEY HECHT

| Zapruder Film Frame 155 | 111 |
| Zapruder Film Frame 197 | 112 |

JAIMEE HILLS

| Chlamydia | 113 |
| Nothing Rhymes with Gitmo | 115 |

KAREN HOLMBERG

| Imago, *Io Moth* | 116 |
| Man o'War | 118 |

LESLEY JENIKE

Against Ornamentation	120
A Rauschenberg Conversation	121
Self-Portrait as the Golden Head at Jardin de Luxembourg	123
A Rothko Conversation	124

CARRIE JERRELL

| The Poet Prays to Her Radio for a Country Song | 125 |
| The Country-Western Singer's Ex-Wife, Sober in Mendocino | |

County, California	126
The Poet Prays to the 9mm under the Driver's Seat	128
The Bridesmaid	129
The Best Man	130
The Maid of Honor	131
When the Rider is Hope	132
I Am Thinking of My First Horse	133
After the Revival	134
When the Rider is Truth	136

ROSE KELLEHER

Ditty	137
Asperger's Muse	138
Zeitoun	139
Neanderthal Bone Flute	140
Impulse	141
Noted Sadomasochists	142
Lye	145
Brockton Man	146
Lovesick	148

DORE KIESSELBACH

The Painted Hall, Lascaux	149
First Hike After Your Mother's Death	150

ELIZABETH KLISE VON ZERNECK

Slant Rhyme	151
Illinois Landscape	152
Science and Industry	154

ANTHONY LACAVARO

An Essay on the Body	155
Babies	156

MATTHEW LADD

Envoi	157
Imitation	158
Poem for K.	159
Scenes From a Common Life	160
Marcel Proust's Last Summer Holiday	166
Klintholm Havn	167
Coelacanth	168

NICK LANTZ

The Year We Blew Up the Whale – Florence, Oregon	169
Gogol's Haircut	171
Challenger	172

JULIE LARIOS

Woman with the Beak of an Octopus	173
Husband, Wife	174

DENNIS LONEY

Flight from the Garden	175
The Man Under the Dump	176

DORA MALECH

Let Me Explain	178

Makeup	179
Delivery Rhyme	180
Here Name Your	182
Push, Pull	184
Drought Year	186
Dreaming in New Zealand	187
A Shortcut	188

CHRISTOPHER TODD MATTHEWS

The Red Balloon (1956)	190
My Impacted Tooth, Never Descended	191
The Roman Baths in June	192

NICOLE MELANSON

The Hunted	193
Becoming Mortal	194

DEREK MONG

Equivalents	195
Re: Vitruvian Man	197
O h i o –	198
Mia	199
Fellini's Satyricon	201
Period	203

SIERRA NELSON

We'll Always Have Carthage	206
Orvieto	207

MICHAEL LEE PHILLIPS

Teaching the Romantics	209
The Man in the Barrel	211
Shooting at Lamar	213

JESSICA PIAZZA

| Kopophobia | 214 |
| Melophobia | 215 |

AARON POOCHIGIAN

| The Marriage of Peleus and Thetis | 216 |
| Kudzu | 217 |

ALISON POWELL

Shangri-La	218
Decorum: A Study	219
Edema	220
The Raw Fields	221

CHRIS PREDDLE

Water Sonnets	222
Not Catullus	225
The Arrowloop	227
Earthmover	228
Ruin	229
First Letter to Ed	230
Cattle Console Him	232
Groundsel	234

BOBBY C. ROGERS

Burning the Walls	235
Nocturne	237
Pastoral	239
Newground	241

JOHN SUROWIECKI

The Hat City After the Men Stopped Wearing Hats	243
Connecticut Invaded by Chinese Communists [1951]	244
The Childless Couple's Child	245
Americanization of a Poem by Wislawa Szymborska	246
The Wisest Aunt, Telling the Saddest Tales	247

MICHAEL SWAN

Not What I Meant	248
How Everything Is	250
Hendrikje Stoffels	251
Some People Get That	252
Lance-Corporal Swan	253

BRADFORD GRAY TELFORD

At the Theatre	254
The Woman Who Was Not Matisse	256
from Excerpts from a Dream House	
The Conversation	258
Regarding a Backsplash	259
Portrait of the Artist's Mother at the Analyst	260
from Four Trees	
Melia azederach	261
September	263
from Self-Portrait on a Need-to-Know Basis	
For Further Information	264

JAMIE JOEL THOMAS

Towing Water to Australia	265
Youth Longs to Live	266

MATTHEW THORBURN

Now is Always a Good Time	267
Horse Poetica	269
Gravy Boat	270
Self-Portrait with Unmentionables	271
Woken Each Morning by the Glad Laughter of Birds	272
Horn of Plenty	273
Still Life	274

D. H. TRACY

The Explorer at Eureka Dunes	276
AWOL	277

BARBARA LOUISE UNGAR

Embryology	279
Riddle	280
Matyroshka	281

CODY WALKER

Update	282
The Cheney Correspondence (Selected)	283
All Poetry is Political	284
Earlier Today, Archival Edition	285
Offenders	286
"The Mold of a Dog-Corpse"	287
Bozo Sapphics	288

Song for the Song-Maker	290
Hephzibah Cemetery / April 1889	291
New Orleans / August 1890	292
Camden / June 1892	293

MIKE WHITE

Invitation	294
Tentacled Motherfucker	295
Wind	296
Age of Miracles	297

LISA WILLIAMS

Gullet	298
Erratics	300
Snow Covering the Leaves of a Magnolia	302

Biographical Notes and Acknowledgments	303
A Note About the Editor	317

The Anthony Hecht Poetry Prize
2005-2009

2005
Judge: J. D. McClatchy
Winner: Morrie Creech, *Field Knowledge*

2006
Judge: Mary Jo Salter
Winner: Erica Dawson, *Big-Eyed Afraid*

2007
Judge: Richard Wilbur
Winner: Rose Kelleher, *Bundle o' Tinder*

2008
Judge: Alan Shapiro
Winner: Carrie Jerrell, *After the Revival*

2009
Judge: Rosanna Warren
Winner: Matthew Ladd, *The Book of Emblems*

Introduction

The Anthony Hecht Poetry Prize, offering a purse of £1,750 or $3,000 and publication in both the United Kingdom and the United States for a first or second volume of poetry, was launched in 2005. This anthology collects poems by fifty of the poets whose work most impressed the readers during the contest's first five years. All of these poems are from manuscripts that were either finalists or semifinalists in the contest: all the finalists are represented here, though not all the semifinalists. There were many other poets, and many other poems, that I would have liked to find space for, but space is of course limited, and difficult choices were necessary, as in the contest. And as in the contest, the selections were not based on any particular criteria concerning style or subject. They simply reflect personal taste, and the desire to represent each of the poets at his or her idiosyncratic best.

It is, as far as I know, unprecedented for a press to publish an anthology of this sort, containing poems by five poets who won its book contest and forty-five who did not. But I believe the quality of the poems gathered here justifies the enterprise, and that readers of this volume will find a strong sample of the best work being done by emerging poets writing in English. Many are young, but not all. More than half of the manuscripts represented here have been published or accepted for publication (the five winners, four others published by Waywiser, and twenty-three taken by other presses), and I am confident that many of the ones that have not yet found a home will find one soon. Despite all the difficulties faced by poets trying to get published these days – more of this in a moment – much, if not all, of the best work does, sooner or later, find its way into print.

When we launched the Hecht Prize, six years ago, we did not know what to expect. We were pleased, and gratified, both by the quality of the manuscripts we received and by their variety. We struggle every year to sort through the hundreds of contestants, some with previous books and many with a very impressive array of magazine credits, to find the ones that seem to us to have the best claim to advance to the final judge. (I should say that although we look at the lists of previous publications, as much out of curiosity as anything, these don't really have an effect on the judging process: one's aesthetic experience of the manuscript quickly takes over, and one forgets the credentials). The final judge, always a poet of stature, receives the eight to ten finalists stripped of all identifying reference. We have been lucky in our judges, who have always made good choices, but we have always felt they had a number of good possibilities to choose from. It is because we have seen so much work of extraordinary quality, so many fine poets whose books deserve to be published, many of which we would have been delighted to publish ourselves had we had the means and opportunity, that we have opted to do more than simply publish the winners. Every year, examples of the work of all the finalists and semifinalists are posted on our website (I know of no other contest that does this). This volume is an extension of that commitment to those we consider the best of our contestants.

That an anthology of this quality could be put together in this way says something both encouraging and disturbing about the state of contemporary poetry. The richness, the variety, the seriousness, the accomplishment evident in the field, every year, is cause for celebration; but it is also troubling to see so many fine poets doing what most poets trying to get established now do: send to contest after contest after contest, year after year after year, in the hope that their manuscript will somehow find its way through the crowd and at last see the light of day. It is a difficult process for the writer, as it often feels a futile if not all but hopeless one, and I don't know whether the excitement followed by disappointment of *coming close* is more heartening or heartbreaking. The proliferation of writing departments and creative writing courses, for all the complaints it has generated of cookie-cutter poetry, has also produced more worthy poets than the traditional mechanisms of publication can accommodate, all the more so as long established houses close their lists to newcomers, or close them down altogether, in deference to the bottom line.

Some numbers may put this in perspective. (These numbers relate to the situation in America, but I don't believe the story they tell is significantly different in the U.K. or other English-speaking countries.) A Library of Congress survey in the 1990s concluded that one out of every twelve Americans writes or has at some point written poetry. Think about that for a moment: in a country of more than three-hundred million, even after subtracting from our calculations the seventy-five million or so under the age of eighteen, that's almost *twenty million* people. Even if only one out of every ten of them does something other than pen the occasional birthday ditty or infrequently jot private musings in a notebook – that is, writes with some regularity and takes it seriously as a part of their life – that's still *two million* of those people. Even if only one out of every ten of *them* has real talent or flair, that's still *two-hundred thousand* of those people, composing at least some poems that merit the attention of magazines and presses. Even if only one out of every ten of *them* has the stamina and fortitude and luck of circumstance necessary to develop that talent, to hone it to a fully realized craft – and now we're getting to the level where the writer deserves some recognition – that's still *twenty thousand* of *those* people. I doubt there is a single reader out there who knows who half of them are. Even if only one out of every ten of *them* has that extra brilliance or genius which elevates craft into art – and now we're at the level where someone who hasn't read them is missing something special – that's still *two thousand* of *those people*. I guarantee you no one has read them all. Some of *those* poets are here.

The reader may of course question my ratios, and he or she is welcome to substitute different descriptions of the levels of the pyramid for the ones that I offer. But I trust my general point is clear. There are too many poets out there for anyone to be confident that they see the whole picture. Our views are all partial, as are our judgments. This unprecedented proliferation is good for contests, setting aside the disorienting labor of sorting through the wild variety of styles and sensibilities, and bad for contestants. Without such a fine excess a volume like this one would be pointless. But given this embarrassment of riches, I would like to think it is revealing, and important, not least as a testimony to artistic persistence in the face of very long odds.

There are many people who are owed thanks for the success the Hecht Prize contest has had over its first five years. First of all there is Anthony Hecht himself, whose generosity to younger poets was exemplary, and who, though he did not live to see it realized, gave his blessing, along with the prestige of his name, to the project. Helen Hecht has remained gracious and supportive throughout.

J. D. McClatchy is owed a double thanks, for his advice to the contest as Anthony Hecht's literary executor, and for his service as our first judge. Our other judges, Mary Jo Salter, Richard Wilbur, Alan Shapiro, and Rosanna Warren, have our deep gratitude as well. I must thank, over his objection, Waywiser's publisher and editor-in-chief Philip Hoy, as well as the other members of our editorial board during the contest's first five years, Clive Watkins and Greg Williamson, whose tireless work and good judgment proved invaluable year in and year out. Heartfelt thanks are owed to Stephen Kampa, Kate Light, Eric McHenry, Joe Osterhaus, and Robert Schreur, who have assisted in the difficult work of reading the manuscripts, and also to Matthew Brenneman, Carla Harrison, and Ed Perlman, for their wise advice when the prize was in its planning stages. Steve Kronen wrote a well-placed article favorable to the press that helped persuade us the time was right to launch the prize. Terri Merz and Steve Moyer of Chapters Bookstore, Barbara Meade and the late Carla Cohen of Politics and Prose Bookstore, and Teri Cross Davis, Janet Griffin, and Steve Enniss at the Folger Shakespeare Library were kind enough to provide the venues where we introduced our winners. The biggest thanks go to our contestants, without whose commitment to the art of poetry, the Anthony Hecht Poetry Prize, and of course this anthology, would not have been possible.

– Joseph Harrison

CRAIG ARNOLD

Incubus

The chain uncouples, and his jacket hangs
on the peg over hers, and he's inside.

She stalls in the kitchen, putting the kettle on,
buys herself a minute looking for two
matching cups for the lime-flower tea,
not really lime but linden, heart-shaped leaves
and sticky flowers that smell of antifreeze.
She talks a wall around her, twists the string
tighter around the teabag in her spoon.
But every conversation has to break
somewhere, and at the far end of the sofa
he sits, warming his hands around the cup
he hasn't tasted yet, and listens on
with such an exasperating show of patience
it's almost a relief to hear him ask it:
If you're not using your body right now
maybe you'd let me borrow it for a while?

It isn't what you're thinking. No, it's worse.

Why on earth did she find him so attractive
the first time she met him, propping the wall
at an awkward party, clearly trying to drink
himself into some sort of conversation?
Was it the dark uncomfortable reserve
she took upon herself to tease him out of,
asking, Are you a vampire? *That depends,*
he stammered, *are you a virgin?* No, not funny,
but why did she laugh at him? What made her think
that he needed her, that she could teach him something?
Why did she let him believe she was drunk
and needed a ride home? Why did she let him
take her shirt off, fumble around a bit
on the spare futon, passing back and forth

the warm breath of a half-hearted kiss
they kept falling asleep in the middle of?
And when he asked her, why did she not object?
I'd like to try something. I need you to trust me.

Younger and given to daydreams, she imagined
trading bodies with someone, a best friend,
the boy she had a crush on. But the fact
was more fantastic, a fairy-tale adventure
where the wolf wins, and hides in the girl's red hood.
How it happens she doesn't really remember,
drifting off with a vague sense of being
drawn out through a single point of her skin
(a bedsheet threaded through a needle's eye)
and bundled into a body that must be his.
Sometimes she startles, as on the verge of sleep
you can feel yourself fall backward over a brink,
and snaps her eyelids open, to catch herself
slipping out of the bed, her legs swinging
over the edge, and feels the sudden sick
split-screen impression of being for a second
both she and her.
                      What he does with her
while she's asleep, she never really knows,
flickers, only, conducted back in dreams:
Walking in neighborhoods she doesn't know
and wouldn't go to, overpasses, ragweed,
cars dry-docked on cinderblocks, wolf-whistles,
wanting to run away and yet her steps
planted sure and defiant. Performing tasks
too odd to recognize and too mundane
to have made up, like fixing a green salad
with the sunflower seeds and peppers that she hates,
pouring on twice the oil and vinegar
that she would like, and being unable to stop.
Her hands feel but are somehow not her own,
running over the racks of stacked fabric
in a clothing store, stroking the slick silk,
teased cotton and polar fleece, as if her fingers

each were a tongue tasting the knits and weaves.
Harmless enough.

                                      It's what she doesn't dream
that scares her, panic she can't account for, faces
familiar but not known, déjà vu
making a mess of memory, coming to
with a fresh love-bite on her left breast
and the aftershock of granting another's flesh,
of having gripped, slipped in and fluttered tender
mmm, unbraided, and spent the whole slow day
clutching her thighs to keep the chafe from fading,
and furious at being joyful, less
at the violation, less the danger, than the sense
he'd taken her enjoyment for his own.
That was the time before, the time she swore
would be the last – returning to her senses,
she'd grabbed his throat and hit him around the face
and threw him out, and sat there on the floor
shaking. She hadn't known how hard it was
to throw a punch without pulling it back.

Now, as they sit together on her couch
with the liquid cooling in the stained chipped cups
that would never match, no matter how hard
she stared at them, he seems the same as ever,
a quiet clumsy self-effacing ghost
with the gray-circled eyes that she once wanted
so badly to defy, that seemed to see her
seeing him – and she has to admit, she's missed him.
Why? She scrolls back through their conversations,
searching for any reason not to hate him,
She'd ask him, What's it like being a girl
when you're not a girl? His answers, when he gave them,
weren't helpful, so evasively poetic:
It's like a sponge somebody else is squeezing.
A radio tuned to all stations at once.
Like having skin that's softer but more thick.
Then she remembers the morning she awoke
with the smear of tears still raw across her cheeks

and the spent feeling of having cried herself
down to the bottom of something. Why was I crying?
she asked, and he looked back blankly, with that little
curve of a lip that served him for a smile.
Because I can't.
                        And that would be their secret.
The power to feel another appetite
pass through her, like a shudder, like a cold
lungful of oxygen or hot sweet smoke,
fill her and then be stilled. The freedom to fall
asleep behind the blinds of his dark body
and wake cleanly. And when she swings her legs
over the edge of the bed, to trust her feet
to hit the carpet, and know as not before
how she never quite trusted the floor
to be there, no, not since she was a girl
first learning to swim, hugging her skinny
breastless body close to the pool-gutter,
skirting along the dark and darker blue
of the bottom dropping out –

                                    Now she can stand,

and take the cup out of his giving hand,
and feel what they have learned inside each other
fair and enough, and not without a kind
of satisfaction, that she can put her foot
down, clear to the bottom of desire,
and find that it can stop, and go no deeper.

BRUCE BERGER

Transmigration

As kerosene climbs through a wick
Or sap through oak by the slow
Fire of transpiration,
So moisture from the saltpan
Has scaled the flesh and feathers
Of this long-fallen crow
And seeded it with crystals.
Alone with its blue shadow
As if on a shield of snow,
Half scavenger with a tough beak,
Now more than half a vessel
That might have served Versailles,
It challenges the sun
With a blistering salt eye,
Easy in the wisdom
That its fellows are nothing at all,
Serene in its lucky fall,
Its dazzling transmigration
From bird to the stabler kingdom
Of the gem and mineral.

Confession

My mother gone eight years,
My father thirty-seven,
The attending physician too old
To find himself at risk:
Now it can be told.

A man I still remember
Flipping onto his hands
And walking that way upstairs,
Spent the latter years
Of my growing up in chairs.

Gymnast, acrobat,
Hellion who retired
And took a second wife
(My mom), golfer, horseman,
Chainsmoker for life,

Sixty when I was born,
Still riding an aquaplane
Around the lake on his head,
He spent the inglorious years
After the chairs in bed.

Self-taught, declaiming Shakespeare,
Kipling and the old chestnuts,
His elocution took off.
I listen for the echo
And only catch the cough.

Of course he blamed the weather.
We traveled where he could breathe.
Bad weather remained his fate.
A doctor made him quit.
Of course it was too late.

He squirted mist in his throat.
Every morning he hacked
Midnight out of his lung.
He wheezed, gasped and offended
Strangers we landed among.

In restaurants, in lobbies,
The clientele complained.
One of the minor hells,
Traveling for better weather,
Was getting kicked from hotels.

Dishonored, oxygen-starved,
The head he used to stand on
Started to forget.
As fully conscioius creatures
We crossed and never met.

Dreamlike, the wit of my childhood.
Then the repeated stories
Of which I retain a store.
By the time I grew into patience
There was less to be patient for.

Then I was off to college;
My mother, thirty years younger
Than he, a nurse in jail;
My father, forever failing,
Failing, failing to fail.

Nights when he gasped at nothing.
Calls to rouse the doctor
Out of bed to sustain
Lifeblood with a shot
Of oxygen straight to the vein,

Just one, for more would kill,
Deliverance enough that Dad
Woke to hack next day.
Fitful letters from Mom,
So little was there to say

Until a sudden call,
Senior year, that my father
Was lost, and I flew back,
The combat with his lung
Resolved by a heart attack.

My mother gone eight years,
My father thirty-seven,
The doctor now so old
He's surely gone as well:
Now it can be told.

Years afterward, my mother
Needed to speak of something
Once and then no more,
But first I had to swear
To secrecy. I swore.

That final breathless night
My mother, frantic, summoned
The doctor to inject
Air in my father's blood.
Now to no effect.

He reached into his bag.
Exaggerating his motions,
Leaving nothing blurred,
He raised a second shot.
Neither breathed a word.

My mother nodded faintly.
The ending came in peace.
The doctor knew the art
Of medicine and wrote
On the death certificate, heart.

But think of your father's family
By his first wife, who hated
The thought of me, and guess
What they just might now
Call me. Murderess.

I wanted you to know
But what I said tonight
Must never be said aloud.
I said I understood
And, furthermore, was proud.

Now she and those she feared
Are gone, or almost gone.
For reasons of my own
I want it known.
I want it known.

PETER BETHANIS

American Future

In 1963 the morning probably seemed harmless enough
for my parents to sign on the dotted line
as the insurance man talked to them for over an hour
around a coffee table about our future.
"This roof wasn't designed to withstand meteors,"
he told my father, who back then had a brush haircut
that made his ears stick out, his moods
still full of passion, willing to listen,
my mother with her beehive hairdo,
smiling back at him, all three of them
wanting so much to make the fine print
of the world work. They laughed and smoked,
and after they led the man politely to the door,

my parents danced in the afternoon light,
the phonograph playing Frank Sinatra,
the green Buick's payments up to date,
five hundred dollars safely in the bank –
later that evening, his infallible common sense
ready to protect us from a burst pipe or dry rot,
my father waded up to his ankles in water,
a V of sweat on the back of his shirt.
Something loomed deeper than any basement
on our block, larger than he was,
an uncertainty he could not admit was unsolvable
with a monkey wrench or a handshake
and a little money down.

The Deer in the Barns

In autumn, the men hang deer
upside down from the barn rafters.
Run their knives the whole length
of the belly – then barrel-hoop their arms
and yank out the guts like a sack of potatoes.
Their eyes tear from the smell
and blood drips down onto newspapers.
Laughing, drinking, talking
late into the night, they gather around the animal,
its eyes blank as bullets, its tongue
a pink glove in its mouth,
its lip curled as if to speak.

One of the sons, rubbing the soft curve
of the deer's ear, asks questions
about death, and once again,
they all huddle about the moonlit dark
with the same sacred lies,
doomed creatures themselves, afraid to flinch.

KIMBERLY BURWICK

Everything Lush I Know

I do not know the names of things,
but I have lived on figs and grapes,
smell of dirt under moon
and moon under threat of rain,
everything lush I know
an orchard becoming all orchards,
flowers here and here
the earth I have left,
every brief home-making,
the lot of God blooming into vines
right now, then, and always.

These Nails, They Point Upwards

You have come here
from the winetree,
the rowantree, the witchwood.
Cherry and apple caskets go
with a soft song to the dead.
The first house you lived in
goes back to thickets.
Wherever we are we are crying for that,
woolgrass brown in firelight,
ground nuts hard as they are.
I want to see what the partridge sees,
scarlet woodbine bright
in the blackish distance.
We are stripped downward,
closely shorn.

My Arrows Are Not Sharp

The real sunlight,
brighter than winter's green,
is the small Bethlehem
we cannot see.
The purblind
and colorblind
are not sainted
but horsewhipped
by wind.
You want to believe
there are bits
of us everywhere,
in the platinum deadwood,
in the widow's
tarnished harvest-home.
But this is abbey-land
and no craven
thing will do

The Norway Tree

This is arcadia
just as this
is a hailstone sun.
I can stand in the gold jasper
volcanic and learn the last words
of wool blowing in wilderness.
As ribs are the ridges
between furrow, you
are the loud-lunged silencer
unsure if I am worth the trouble.
Plant me in the mountain
of the heart's mutilation,
spinster me, my maple.
I can wait hours for you
to change one leaf.

Must One Wait For It to Wither?

Each horse is the one I leave at the cathedral
at the beginning of the story.
The animals on your farm do not comfort me
the way I am.
My stomach twists and does not untwist.
Each animal is the abstraction
that goes through me.
I want to say that wheat feels the same
as a whole house lifting or calm is the caw
at the center of carnage.
But wheat is still wheat from the
window painted shut. Winter ahead is
a cold-front with snow.
You want to know if I go back.
If he has eaten the patches of blue and yellow
alpine flowers, if I untie him or simply stroke
the back of his neck. I cannot say anything
but the horse is calm is black and made sad by the storm.

MICHAELA CARTER

The Debutante Ball

After the father-daughter waltz
has folded to a close,
she sheds the white weight
of Grandmother's kid gloves,
seventeen embroidered eyelets,
buttons (mother-of-pearl);
starry stockings; slips; wedding gown
missing its train. White filigreed bra.

By earliest amber, her escort
kills the engine in a cloud of roadside dirt.
Front seat nearly flattens as she yanks
its lever all the way up.
Ever the flirt, she soils hastily –
a touched gardenia.
Her imagination smirks at last,
and browns like a stain. . . .

Beauty never could resist the spindle's
prick.
      Under all her graces,
she needed pain.

When We Speak of Love

We never use it as a verb, not if *I*
is the subject and *you* the object. Instead

when morning falls in bars of sky
or water blue across the bed,

you close the blinds, pull me to your chest
and I slide back inside

the dream where there are seconds left,
seconds before the stretch of low tide

is gone with my breath, your heart, a clock,
a time bomb, as the wave crests, black,

and skyscraper high. We should talk –
discuss *us* – I guess. But the wave's wake

is a mile of water I am under,
a mile of silver, breathless wonder.

KEN CHEN

My Father and My Mother Decide My Future and How Could We Forget Wang Wei?

The suitcase
open on the bed. My grandfather is packing up
his organs. This completed, he takes a taxi to my grandmother's
house for supper. Exits
the empty car to Taipei alley.

Dissolve. Now the Los Altos lot.

So did you listen to him, MY FATHER says taking his keys out of the ignition. You should
become a lawyer but your grandfather says anything is fine. As long as
you're the best.
    MY FATHER stays, MY MOTHER stays silent. I sit and suck my thumb.
I saw your painting. It was beautiful, my mother says to WANG WEI, restrained
behind us by backseat-belt and streetlight world – WANG WEI who says:

> In the silent bamboo woods, sitting along
> Playing strings and bellowing long.

But America is allergic to bamboo, MY FATHER to WANG WEI. They love skill sets, cash and
the first person singular, the language of C++ not our English. Steps out, shuts the
door, puts gas pump by Acura trunk. My father's son does not understand, forgets the
Chinese he never remembered. But my mother holds words in her mouth:
    The Peking opera soundtrack of my childhood. You sound

like it. I'd listen to it on the
radio. You know, when I had to sweep the floor. And then WANG
 WEI:

> Nobody knows but the deep grove
> and the luminous moon that glows in response.

California moon not glow – or as the translation might say,
 irradiates instead like
beige screen before MY MOTHER, now at HP, after Taipei and
 degree in Home Ec.
and divorce. MY MOTHER like the moon which rents light from
 its past, MY MOTHER
who says, looking at the dashboard, You should listen to your
 father. I don't know. Here
he comes.
MY FATHER unlocks the door and says, Dropped the keys in the
 toilet. But that's what life is
like. You're young, MY FATHER says, I'm not sure to me or
 WANG WEI, You don't understand the
world, the world which loves those who enter it and then WANG
 WEI:

> Red hearts in the southern country
> Spring comes with stems enlarging.
> I didn't know you two were still together.

We're not, MY FATHER says. You're eavesdropping on my son's
 unwaking life.
 Your son? WANG WEI of monochromatic line turns behind
holds seat-strap with left hand and asks talk-show serenely: Who
 are you?

He has seen me. Like the scene
in the movie, where the actors find the camera and say Stop
looking at me, they stand and quit the car the way a breeze
 would. And I say:

> Wish you'd gather some, caught me

More of this thing that is longing.

And Wang Wei asks: Who are you?
And my Father says: Decide.

SCOTT COFFEL

Light-Years from My Redemption

Catholic in my envy, I crucified every rival –
the satyr, the encyclopedist, the dwarf
Apollo with his rhythm sticks, the diplomat with his pimp's eye
for local talent and Gerard, that non-practicing
atheist with his transuranic lisp and ties to the Vatican.
All for the love of Horst (her nickname since childhood)
who taught me German and other delicacies of Middle Earth
in a railroad flat off Second Avenue,

light-years from my redemption on Mount Rushmore,
the pines tipped with fire as I perused the face of free will
blasted into the granite text of *The Critique of Pure Reason* –
my mind losing opacity, skidding past its music
into deep space where the Big Bang, enfeebled by expansion,
bleated like an act of grace in sheep's clothing.

In the Throes of Advanced Study

In 1970 I penetrated the insular world of the Skelquetons,
a tribe whittled down to twenty souls and three acres
of black flies deep in the Adirondacks, where the golden
logos of the inner thigh was reserved for mystics gasping

in the throes of advanced study. Beginners like myself
were tortured, chiefly by means of sensual deprivation,
given nothing of the body but the esoteric growth of hair
south of a woman's knuckle. One week with the Skelquetons

encompassed years of adolescent anguish. Nothing I did
pleased them; they were intemperate judges, brutal horses
of instruction, all my rebellions of thought were crushed
and letters of reprimand mailed home to my widowed mother.

It was humiliating and senseless, much like the year 1970
itself, with its crew-cut Wagnerians in the White House
scrimmaging for power with a German Jew: year of the dead
and paralyzed students, the fog of repellant and war.

Andrei and Natasha

In a blow to Marxist thought, our romance red-shifted
from farce to tragedy. I had the paper trail to prove it,
a receipt from the erotic bakery with your phone number
and testimonial to the doctrine
of mutually assured orgasm. The Days of Awe were at hand
and I was grateful for something to atone for.
Years and two lovers apart, we kissed goodbye, nostalgic
for the future as rain speckled our trench-coats.

The Russian winter came early to New York State.
Though corrupted by property and jealous of your freedom
I accepted your collect call, amalgamating
phone sex with *War and Peace*, my life-thwarted prince
dying in your arms as the Anti-Christ reached Oneonta,
the City of the Hills where love began and ended.

Cockeyed Louie

In the welfare state of heaven the pamphlets promise
that even cockeyed Louie with his glum Chihuahua,
with the lewd postcard in his pocket
and the Hebrew god on his tongue, with his forty years of drudgery
and his cramped apartment next to the incinerator chute
and his trips to the Food Fair taking hours for a bag
of peppers and light bulbs and toilet paper and dog food,
that even he shall know an end

to the injustice and the carnage
and the boredom: cockeyed Louie, who blessed
the sanctity of unions on summer nights under the vapor-lamps,
cursing the rich while his irritated dog squeaked at mosquitoes:
cockeyed Louie,
who wept for my father at the synagogue, who kept his distance
after Labor Day, whose clothes grew fearfully loose by November,
who by April had disappeared entirely.

Emerald City

I'll thunder Blake's "Jerusalem" until Security drags me feetfirst
from this corporate lavatory, my ten stolen minutes of
>   the imagination
doused forever, having consumed nothing but the smallest
denomination of company time, for which my punishment
will be too lenient to bear.

Forgive my soul's incontinence, the sky stained
east to west from an experiment gone awry with vials of copper
>   sulfate,
dusk over the opera house
as I push the envelope of decorum with offstage hernia coughs
during a performance of *Tannhauser*. Dying here

is to suffer from a rare form of health, to watch the Space Needle
emptied of its vaccine, the mind inoculated against pandemics of
>   reality.
To die here is to learn what is learned where others live –
that the end is dark as our friends are false, that even lovely hills
harbor gas pipes belching fire.

Hordes of Indigent Psychologists

Hours after my decision to defect, the elders of the West
blamed me for the drought and the power failure. Monopolists at
    heart,
it was they who gouged the price of remaining
to prohibitive levels. I've outgrown the sequoia. I've ogled
my last Joan of Arc at the drive-in *auto da fé*.

Time to release my daemon on its own recognizance,
to resuscitate my dream of staging *The Ring* cycle in its original
    Yiddish
or inciting riots among hordes of indigent psychologists
practicing in squalor under the viaduct.

Bald as my tires, I haven't hugged the road in years.
But why disclose my lusts to gluttons for titillation?
Better to misread a cluster of thunderheads building
east of Des Moines for the tops of the Olympic Mountains, my life
at forty beginning *in medias res* of a price war between rival
    masseuses.

Mild Worlds Elsewhere

I thought of Santayana, doomed as I was
        to repeat my long history of selling myself short
during an interview with a German publishing house

    for a job I had no intention of accepting.
        Given a youth's revulsion
to old age, how could I, a stripling of twenty-seven, spend

    the last years of my Roman adolescence
        mired in the nomenclature of bodily decrepitude,
seeing the face of Yeats emerge from a water stain

    on the 14th floor of the Flatiron Building,
        the moist eyes of Personnel
reflecting my textbook case of dread as it shuddered through me,

    my legs damp behind the knees,
        my mind split into opposing camps
of self and soul: always two places at once should IRA terrorists

    detonate a pound of Semtex under the immense
        remainder bins at the Strand Bookstore
or should the rebbe Schneerson rise from his grave in Queens

    waving fistfuls of strange wisdom.
        To be somewhere for one's self is hard enough
but to be there for others in the guise of a useful citizen

    is to knit
        low-necked sweaters with the femurs of a saint,
to shake the inquisitor's hand while hydrogen fuses into helium

    over the Devil's Tower of 23rd Street and dream
        of mild worlds elsewhere,
far-off rondures of the universe where the fossil fuels of evil

are depleted, the glassworks
            in ruins, the human-sized jars shattered,
where the flight from God is neither down nor across but up

      into a fake Bavarian village
            with its twin scourges of ultraviolet and trail mix:
verboten to the ones who congregate at sea level,

      where the bookshelves of every household
            are floating wonders of faith and knowledge,
filled with the weightlessness of Swedenborg and Isaac Luria,

      where the rebbe never reaches
            the end of his day as a human being,
resting with one eye open in the dark hours measled with light.

ANDREW COX

Two Plus Two Equals Five

And so a toy drum equals a Saturday Night Special,
a boy grows up to be a foot doctor, a little girl
subtracts yes from no and lives out the sum,
multiplying it by minus one on her death bed,
saying, "yes, father, I'm coming, don't leave me,"
while a stuffed rabbit equals a lingering good-bye,
good-bye to the one face we'll never see again,
except in the past (that string unwinding behind us,
because you'll never know when you'll have to go back)
and so one wedding gown (packed in mothballs
in a cedar chest in an attic) divided by a field
(blanketed by snow and unmarred by footsteps)
equals a fierce longing and yet, for what, the man
who talks to himself can't say, only that it has
something to do with frost-bitten feet and someone
who plays a flute and someone who beats a drum
and many marching forward, always forward
and slightly out of step, always…and so one broken nose
equals the scar from triple bypass surgery and the return
to a simple way of life, if we could only get there,
if we could only find that perfect mattress
on which to flop, the perfect soap for washing off
the day's residue, the perfect moment to unveil
our new hope in the equation that explains everything.

The American Museum

"There's a sucker born every minute." – P.T. Barnum

The Swedish Nightingale gave
performances there, as did
the General, the Feegee Mermaid,
the Siamese twins, Chang and Eng
(who hated each other: imagine that,
joined at the shoulder to your despised
identical opposite), the bearded lady
who went to court to prove
she wasn't a man, and Jumbo,
poor Jumbo, passed off as
the world's largest pachyderm,
smashed to his death
by a train – the fact is
most entertainment comes
at someone's expense. Think of it,
a moment's escape and how much
we pay for it, how much we need
a reprieve, to stop the flow
of information long enough
to watch another freak: a joker
who dons bat ears and calls himself
the Caped Crusader.
From eating out
to the extravagant love for a pet,
we fight off that dreaded foe
boredom. In this war
there's never enough sensation, never enough
diversion, never enough to keep us
from coming back to ourselves,
up late watching a movie because we can't sleep,
going over and over again
some minor mishap of the day
that exposes us to the one fear

we can't swallow: that everything
they say about us
is true. It's all true.

MORRI CREECH

World Enough

Swift as a weaver's shuttle, time unspools
    its hours in glistening threads
and rapturous polychromes – in the arc of leaf
    or feather toward the pools
of that deep shade to which the morning weds
    its brilliance, in a brief

slur of redwings above the white-washed fence,
    the sprinkler's lisp and hiss
trailing a veil of diamond through the air –
    and spins a present tense
of such dizzying concords one is apt to miss
    much of the affair.

Think of those vast histories that have gone
    unnoticed or unseen:
ants marching on some martial expedition,
    defending their Babylon
of mounds and chambered catacombs between
    the posts of the Crucifixion,

bees building their honey in the walls
    at Jericho or Troy –
whole catalogs of kingdoms and empires,
    straw-built citadels,
Spenglerian cycles of health and slow decay,
    all lost in the spangled fires

of daylight, the rich flux of hours and years.
    Amid such dense detail
it's easy to miss the moment when Atropos
    bends close with her shears
to cut the taut threads, until their tensions fail
    and time's grip turns loose;

easy, in Eden's commerce of sunlight,
    wild fruit and stippled wings,
to miss the cormorant bristling on the bough.
    So once a man lost sight,
near Pompeii, of history's beginnings,
    caught in some lavish *now*

of appetite – the flush of sex, the steam
    rising from his bathwater –
in all that languor failing to note the wind
    stir the trickled streams
along his flanks, the mountain sound its thunder,
    or those first warm snows descend.

The Canto of Ulysses

Primo Levi, in his apartment in Turin, reading *The Divine Comedy*. February, 1987

Drowsing, head propped above the eighth circle,
he feels the present shifting like a keel,
takes his bearings by the toss and swivel

of snow in window light – though still less real,
it seems to him, than that thick Polish snow
which, tumbling in his mind, begins to wheel

like Dante's leaves or starlings, like the slow
stumble of shades from an open freight car,
or from an open book. All night, the snow

whirls at his window, whiting out the stars.
We sailed now for the stars of that other pole.
Leafing a thumb-worn page, he tries to parse

those lines he once struggled to recall
for a fellow prisoner, who'd hoped to learn
Italian as they scraped rust from the wall

of an emptied petrol tank. *The greater horn
began to mutter and move, as a wavering flame
wrestles against the wind and is overworn –*

although, oddly enough, the lines sound tame
now there is no one to explain them to.
Nor words to write. His own canticle of pain

is, after all, finished. The past is nothing new.
And the present breaks over him like the dream
of firelight, plush eiderdown, and hot stew

a prisoner will sometimes startle from
who has lost hope of returning to the world,
blowing upon his hands the pluming steam

MORRI CREECH

of breath, in which a few snowflakes are whirled.
Or, nodding above the passage where Ulysses
tells how the second journey ended – hurled

by a *fierce squall,* till *the sea closed over us* –
he feels at the moment like that restless king
home from Troy after twenty years, his face

grown old and strange from so much wandering,
who broods all night over the cyclops' lair
or Circe's pigs, the shades' dim gathering,

then falls asleep.
                He leans back in his chair.
It all seems now just like it seemed – the snow;
the frozen dead. They whisper on the stair

as if he'd called their shades up from below
to hear the story of Agamemnon slain,
or paced out the long maze of the *Inferno*

to hear their lamentations fresh again.
Beyond his window: stars, the sleeping town,
the past, whirled like flakes on a windowpane –

the sea closed over us, and the prow went down.
Dreaming, he drops the book without a sound.

For the Rebel Angels

Heaven is a casino. Bright. No clocks.
Everyone strikes it rich on the rigged machines.

But a few would like to find out what it means
to come up short, crap out, to take hard knocks.

They've known too long the splendor of Pure Being.
The booze they drink has no effect at all.

But some would like to stumble drunk, to fall
down on a cocktail girl and grab her wings.

They whisper out of earshot of the pit boss.
Each one shuffles a deck tucked in his feathers.

They're talking odds, they're shrugging off the tethers
of a sure thing, they're weighing risk and loss.

The rakish haloes slump in the swank light.
They shed a few bronze quills and make their way.

Now each of them sleeves a card and starts to play.
With luck, they may lose everything tonight.

The Resurrection of the Body

for Keith Carter

Not quite, I think, what the pious would have prayed for,
these bodies flayed and hived to such permanence –
but you should know that in Florence, down a long corridor
smelling of beeswax, formaldehyde, and dust, a room opens
onto the afterlife. Past skulls arranged and numbered
in the pristine chambers of the ossuary, past jarred infants
pickled in suspension, dwarf limbs brined and labeled word for word
in that dead language sacred to God and science,
you are permitted at last to enter upon that hall
alone, without a guide, to commit the casual sacrilege
of looking. You should keep silent there among the cells,
the treasuries of glass catacombs, if you would gauge
their mysteries, would make out the faintly audible hum
like an angel's labored breath, the stir of seraphic wings
pressing against the stone door of a tomb
not emptied but transfigured, or like the murmurings
of bees, a sound that is merely the current's
dull surge through fluorescent lights blazing overhead
and gusts of cold air from the hundred vents
that preserve and tend the chambers of the dead.

Down that hall which opens on such depths of understanding
as memory cannot plumb within the soul,
twinned heads, their occipitals fused together, hang
Janus-faced above fleams and styptics, forceps and bone chisels,
and the corpse whose legs are swollen to balloons
stands propped beside a text of scriptured flesh, the flesh made word
in a long series of two-inch thick incisions –
cleaned, cross-sectioned and neatly drained of blood,
then wedged between panes of the clearest glass,
pages in which are pressed the layered revelations
of sinew and ligament, lymph nodes, lungs and pancreas,
the nerves' branchwork, down to the knotted rosary of spine;
but if you keep moving, careful not to loiter among the viscid
relics, vanities of those who hoped the intellect

could reach the end of that unending road,
if you look ahead, your attention fixed
on distant archways and ever-opening chambers,
you will reach a place where every light is muted,
dimmed on these wax revenants writhing in postures
of breached ecstasy. Each figure here was resurrected
from hundreds of dissections, hundreds of anonymous
subjects who believed the body is immortal,
would be raised again from the corpse-seed, the dross
of blood and marrow, not from the emptied cells
of honey bees, their combs melted to fill
plaster molds of exposed viscera,
then shaped to the martyred gestures of these models
gazing back from the dust of a different era –

think of Bartholomew prone beneath the blade,
saints so wedded to their pain
the reward for unerring faith seems paid
with each sweep of the knife, the shrill refrain
of metal scoring bone; or conquered Marsyas,
body drawn from its sheath, peeled from the swaddling-bands
that death unwinds. One form still displays
its cut and raveled skin draped from an outstretched hand,
the other hand clutching the bloodied knife.
A woman extends full length on her divan,
arm thrown back in the languor of spent desire, true to life
except for the skull uncorked to expose the brain,
the dermal mask bisected, so that if you leaned close
enough, you could reach your hand inside
the wound, trace each branch along the lymphatic pathways,
could believe the furrowed bone, the blood's halt tide,

but you should take care. Though this is a medical museum,
where every niche and chamber is consecrated
to certainties – each looped intestine, each limb
and cancered torso indexed, catalogued, and dated –
though cell to synapse we know the woof and texture
of human tissue, science will not explain
the swarm of immensities raging there

beyond the precincts of lens or lancet, explain
this ravaged flesh redeemed in wax
twisted to the postures of the living, nor account for why
centuries after the bone saws and scalpels extracted
the tender briskets, their forms compel the eye –
science does not account for why our gaze
lingers on the flayed resurrections of another age
long after the mind has gleaned from their hived bodies
the honey of knowledge.

Listening to the Earth

after the photograph by Robert ParkeHarrison

We'd heard the prophets speak,
knew well their eloquent thunder, the split stone
and urgent whirlwind of their voice and word,
had grown used to the fierce synaptic streaks
of flame, the olive-bearing birds
and withered fields that figured their concern.

But what we'd never heard
was their silence: the wind grown inarticulate
at their retreat from us, the god's command
hushed in the trees – a voice they'd said had stirred
for our ears that we might understand
what now, plainly, none of us could interpret.

At first we were relieved;
such talk of mystery and consequence
when there was work to do, laundry and errands,
the grain waiting for harvest. So we lived
unhindered for a while, our minds
less cluttered, clearer, fixed in the present tense.

But who would read the hail,
storms and stars, the pale fever of winter sun
or those first harsh winds that flushed the moon's gold,
swept the corn and mellowed the plums each fall?
Who was there to say what the world
meant? The raven's flight, bees sweetening carrion,

had little to do with us;
the sparrow's note was foreign to our ears.
Breezes stirred in the eaves much as before,
it seemed, but kept on saying less and less
about us. On the granary floor
the scattered chaff would not speak to our fears.

It wasn't the god we missed,
but how a god might sound, those metaphors
and tropes that yoked us to some vast design,
threshing hidden shades up out of the mist,
or lilies that neither toil nor spin,
beneath a sky now strewn with random stars.

And in the plain streets we listened
for those syllables that once conjured the cold,
fathomless swells of Leviathan-haunted seas,
the fabled bush ablaze on hallowed ground,
and snowflakes' mythic treasuries
transfiguring our ordinary fields.

Firstfruits

> *But now is Christ risen from the dead,*
> *and become the firstfruits of them that slept.*
> – Corinthians 15:20

You've heard it before, I'm sure,
how the vault of heaven will strew its vital gold
a thousand pieces, bright as an angel's gown
    in the sweet, consummate hour
when all that the saints and prophets have foretold
comes true: the dead raised up, each mortal coil
    wound firm on the spindled bone,
and love at last unbounded by despair
    or the grave confines of soil.

    Rumors have often bred
in choir lofts, barber shops, on the front steps
of the local five and dime – how Pee Wee Gaskins,
    now locked in his cell, was said
to have killed at least a hundred, how the tulips
on the church lawn one morning were seen to blaze
    gold with the lucent skins
of five copperheads: till everyone agreed
    these were the final days.

    Or so it seemed that summer
When floodtides razed the coast. You've read, of course,
that flesh is bare grain, like unto a seed,
    that no one knows the hour
of the Lord's design – but storm winds gathered force,
blasting the rain against the window glass,
    steeping the lawns to mud,
and even those of us who lived this far
    inland could hear the toss

    and whiplash of tall pines,
steeples plucked from churches, the hiss of downed wire.
Still, who could have predicted what we'd wake to?
    Not even Pee Wee Gaskins
brooding over his strangled girls could conjure
what lay in the light that gilded one soaked field,
    lay strewn beneath a rainbow
spanning the far pasture when the last rains
    hushed. It was not the world

    we hoped for. There they were,
the dead returned as we had never known them
in life, some kneeling against a fallen tree
    or face down in the water,
washed from the graves to constitute their kingdom;
and, sun-touched near the pasture's edge – *O Death*
    where is thy victory,
thy sting? – an infant swaddled in coils of fence wire,
    snagged on a harrow's teeth.

GREGORY CROSBY

from The Court of Erros

I

You ... & then went down, his ship. To begin?
Cock in hand, as good a place as any, Frank's
oiled hand on his rudder, Frank the navigator
beneath his constellations. Stars, his pin-ups.
Stroke, counted off like a galley slave, heart
thudding like a drum, he could laugh to beat

the band. The starlight like a map of joy,
firecrackers suspended in their exploding.
Strung out, far away, yet they are his guide:
Frank the mariner, adrift, in love with his
sextant, his courses without destinations,
where there is nothing extant of his voyages

but the swell, like a curving thigh, of waves,
one after another, himself his own voyeur.
Isn't that enough, sailor? The pleasure of storms,
the delight of shipwrecks, the unchanging
horizon? Limitless, Frank cresting, he thinks,
Yes, and *yes*, and *yes*. And *no*. No.

XVII.

In sleep, nothing forgotten; insomnia,
nothing forgiven, not even this. Curled,
naked, on top of the covers, waiting to
wake in one's own skin, even if icy at
3 or 4am. Too warm or too worn?
The Emperor's new hairshirt

is unseen, real enough. Look how he
bleeds from the cuffs. Curled, a shaving
from some larger block of existence,
some way of being shaped by scraping,
a hardness gouging, an undressing.
Undressed, Frank refuses to unmake

the bed he has made (or sleep in it).
Conjures a demon lover, fresh from below
to keep him warm, wills it, can almost feel
the enveloping, the blistering embrace,
Shadrach in the furnace. *Hold me*, he says;
spooning, medicine & sugar at once.

XLII.

This thing of darkness, I:
a role, labyrinthine, played as best as can.
Beneath gray and white, waiting for the
Renaissance to raise its hoary head, dead
leaves in its hair. Hey nonny, non.
Five years, the Globe returns,

to mock and occupy the same place:
a stone thrown into an Emerald Pool
(like a heart it sank). Four before that,
the stone she plucked from the Virgin River
that met his thumb: the pricking yet,
the skin calling for its worry. What, me?

Someone would relish your worst luck.
What care do you need wear away – this day,
a cloud that moves, moves & never bursts
in the worn faces of these ghosts, ghosts,
waiting to be born. Past or future, non:
acknowledge, mine.

ERICA DAWSON

Nappyhead

I was born, Mom says, Afro-
Ready, a doll with woman's hair,
Born eight-ball bald between two bare
Legs now long grown, and, Oh

Baby, born with an infant's beard,
Lanugo blonde on tan – so fine
And Foxy Brown circa 1979
In a christening gown. Head smeared

With Lustrasilk, I wore
Six black-girl ponytails, barrettes
In geo-shapes and the alphabet's
Small caps, head dressed and more

Power to me. Parts
Curved with the scalp ran left and right
In a twice-crossed crucifix. At night,
The braids went loose. For tart's

Sake, I went red, called it
An accident then dyed my eye-
Brows too. I said I'd prettify
My lashes, benefit

From the cheap mascara wand
In purple-pink with fake strands glued
To mine – blue streaks, new attitude,
And eighties' chic *beau monde*.

If I cut more than a few
Short strands, Mom saved them in a bag
As a memento. Last year's shag
Smelled sweet with grease and shampoo,

And dried like paper, dead
Confetti kept in an envelope
With blood-stained baby teeth, jump rope,
And a sailor dress. I said

I'd make a wig – bouffant,
Bardot, big bang, and, man, that James
Brown pageboy's fly, man, *fly!* The dame's
Chignon- or debutante-

French twist – I've been the priss
Plucked hard, hot-waxed until the skin
Bubbles, straightened before the thin
Locks break beneath the hiss

And curling iron's steam.
I'm bleached, but call me Nappyhead,
And know that one week after I'm dead
The roots still grow, shea cream

And pomade gone, the bare
Legs freckled with follicles, the shaved-clean
Pussy's five-o'clock shadow, the Queen
Bee, now not worth a hair.

Doll Baby

I was born, Mom says, by the Slice-
N-Tug, Cesarean, just hand-
Picked like a toy from a trunk – God-tanned
And yet, *transparent?* ice-

Blue cord choking a hold
Around my neck. I convalesced
In incubator sheen, undressed
And darling, I've been told.

From preemie small, I grew
Past grown ("Goddamn Incredible Hulk.")
I'm too-short pants and breasts, all bulk,
And nipple peek-a-boo,

Barbie, and Glamour Do.
I'm Elegance. I've seen mom's scar,
And *my* stretch mark of *rouge et noir*,
The pubescent residue

From the navel down, from where
I grew – my pigment's treasure trail
Like bristle on an alpha male.
But am I debonair

Since someone told me once,
"You're big enough to be a man" –
Adam in Eve, all Dapper Dan
And Dressy Bessy? Once,

Twice, three times a lady? Yes,
Me tall? Yes. Model-like I'll lie
In a Da Vinci sprawl (*fee fi ...*)
And feminine finesse.

I'm Stretch. I'm doll-like seams
Inside and out. My brain's in two
Halves split again. *In transitu*
My veins shoot blood in beams

Of brilliant red, the red
Of airbrushed lips, of toy-faced cheeks.
I'll flirt in flush because Clinique's
On sale. I'll lie in bed

Made-up, a daydream death
With playtime *rigor mortis*, id stiff
In still-life poise, and watch my midriff
Rise, and hear one last breath.

Post mortem, Mommy's prize
Will close her eyes and (finally) abstain,
The Porcelain Princéss, the Chatelaine
Dwindling to average size.

OCD

The learned men call it all a true
Emergency, the summer's long,
Tireless drought. And I walk through
The public park breaking the thong
Of my flat flip flop, limping in strong,
Gross heat while the proletariat
Of honey-suckle wilts along.
Quod me nutrit me destruit.

When Death strolls past, what will they do,
The pussy-willows in the throng
Of goldenrod turned brown, but cue
The organ, its sepulchral song
In desiccating sun, grow long
And tall in soil, fertile, fit?
The bell will toll – one loud ding-dong.
Quod me nutrit me destruit.

Deep in the trees, two schoolboys chew
On grass and toss their homemade bong
Inside a bag when I step through
The bush. The smell of smoke is strong.
They stay with me, wading the long
Path of the littered rivulet.
Without a clue, they nod along.
Quod me nutrit me destruit.

I always know where I belong.
Lock all the gates. I'm desperate
To hear birds sing my constant song,
Quod me nutrit me destruit.

Credo

As a woman, I have learned
Some men are really bad

At whispering, as if
Their tenors can't be tempered,

Slight winds, perhaps, more apt
At fine seduction. Still,

Give me their manly lows,
The broader pitch of *Os*,

Pharynx tremors, and hard
*G*s. Now I've come to think

Their throats are coated red,
Bright red, engorged, a sinew

Of veins across their necks
When they inflect a sound

And swallow, understood.
Though something should be said

For breath, an *h* unseen
In *God*, lipped in *Come here*,

My mouth is big. I think
I'm ready for my manhood.

Parallax

Icicles plummet from the porch and sow
Drips, prisms, rainbows, daggers celestial
In their own right. They're lit with touch-and-go
Low beams. The moon slices residual
Storm clouds. Kaleidoscopes, the crystals crack
Colorless on the concrete and land in black.
You stare that black *more* black until the three
Branches across the street from a broken tree
Lose edges, shape, and still the vantage – last
Before you sleep. Through hedges you can see.
The train is coming slow and coming fast.

The later it gets, the more the sky will glow
In a strange reversal. Immaterial,
The stars are hidden in the indigo
Turning to rose, pinks so prophetical
Of sunny days – our nightly almanac.
And on the quarry lake the mallards quack.
Drakes lift and soar as if they're willowy
Feathers. A squawking goose attempts to flee
Their noise. He flaps his wings in the water's blast
Of droplets rising from the ice debris.
The train is coming slow and coming fast.

The more you sleep, the harder it is to throw
The nightmare off yourself, with its optical
Illusion and your eyes closed. Then, with no
Vision, your every where is visual.
I had a soundless dream once, saw the smack
Of cedar switches, saw the sting on black
Limp bodies, like spring blooms, hanged delicately
From a bough, strange fruit, decaying canopy
Of shade. I picked each one. One laughed at me.
He mouthed, blue-lipped, *We'll fall eventually.*
The train is coming slow. And coming fast,

The wind-blown icicles and jagged snow
Knock at my door, alive, no, visceral
As scraping fingernails, and the curio
Skyline moves like a shaken snow globe full
Of glittered flakes inside their hands. *We're back.*
Now let us in. The taps won't stop. I pack
My ears with tissue. *Yeah, those drapes could be*
Your noose. You're history. Yes, you. Go free –
But no – *sputter and snap. Look on, aghast.*
Go on, and gag on your own gravity –
The train is coming slow and coming fast:

What parallax (seesawing winks, the grow,
The shrink, the aweing always temporal,
The voices, mine). I see the train tracks show
Straight as a V. The lights bear destinal,
An oversight on dirt and the growing stack
Of branches. It seems they'll never shine where the track
Meets street and the land spreads constant, flat, a free
Expanse of time and space. Consistently
The horn blows louder, clearer, breezes gassed
With fumes when the red eyes start to flash. Fuck me.
The train is coming, slow and coming. Fast ...

Swing low ... the arm comes down. Illusory,
The scene melds quick as prose and poetry,
And I take it all in, still, as a metaphrast.
Pied Piper, play that piccolo; tell me
The train is coming slow and coming fast.

Bees in the Attic

When to the sessions of sweet silent thought
I summon up remembrance of things past
– William Shakespeare

As if I'd move enough to make a noise
As loud as theirs, those bees, I circled around
My whirring bedroom, hurdling children's toys.
I thought my lungs would buzz the attic's sound,

Crescendo, *shh* and hum; went round until
I lost my breath, lay down. The ceiling wet,
White dark with the hive, I dreamt the comb would spill
Its honey on my pink blankets. When it met

My lips the plaster lath would crack, and sweet
Dead bees stuck to the stucco shards would swarm
My face. I'd drown in wings and the petite
Menagerie with the giant verve. So, warm

And wrapped, I moved the covers, stood on my toes
And reached, and to this day nobody knows

I reached. And to this day nobody knows
The stucco's crimson dot came from my tongue.
When helping Mom in our small kitchen, I flung
The spinach-water and the afterflows

Of faucet-drips with flicking fingers, throws
To the fogged window above the sink. They clung,
I waited, for seconds until the window wrung
Itself of green, steam tears and the glass sang the woes

Of hissing chicken thighs fried in the cast
Iron pot. And the window sang in Grandma's voice,
"Go Down, Moses," and the stained-glass sugar plum

Fairy that hung on the liquid pane at the last
"My people go," raised up her hands. "Rejoice!"
I heard the bees from there growl in a hum.

From there, I heard the bees growl in a hum
Everywhere, in Sylvan lilacs that I picked
For the basement's dollhouse, singing in the drum-
ming dryer's pulse as the washer flowed and clicked.

Their noise was huge to the pint-sized figurines
Who had no ears, but eye-shaped mouths. I posed
Their arms and legs in small domestic scenes
Of "Daddy's home," their tiny red door closed,

Their eye-mouths always open in a gasp
Or scream, as if something were about to fall
Upon their house like the locust plague. The hasp
Was fastened tight. I knocked them down, played all

Four died before the darkness could descend
As if, somehow, I'd write their perfect end.

As if somehow I'd write the perfect end
To every moment, tonight, outside my house
Long left behind, I watch a hydrant douse
A child. And when I let the darkness bend

Around me in a blink, I fade to black.
Eyes closed, I eulogize the Harbor's dock,
Old Bay, the lit-up Bromo-Seltzer clock
Blue in the smoke from the beacon, the factory stack,

Night's quasi-black against the smoke's bright white.
The voice inside my head is talking smack.
The coda of today is just tonight,
No climax, only here and the bric-a-brac

Of memories just fond in retrospect.
In them, the spring's azaleas genuflect.

In them, that spring, azaleas genuflect,
Wilting, about to die in our little garden;
The noon sun bores too hot; sweat droplets harden
And case my cheeks as new weeds bottleneck

The ants in sidewalk cracks. That spring, I cried
And checked and checked in mania. I died
My hardest but it never took. No doubt
I didn't have the guts to try. But I'd scout

Locations (tool shed? shower? tub?), and Dad
And Mom, in separate rooms, would sleep right through
My tiptoed wandering about our blue,
Big siding house. I settled on the plaid

Of my own sheets, penning the letter in
My head. It pounded with adrenaline…

It pounds in my head with my adrenaline.
Dear Mom,
*   Call me the dummy, the mannequin,*
Dead as the dancer in the box that sings
The Mendelssohn on the top shelf and rings
With the scope of bells, and vibrates with the sound
Of clocks. The clock ticks loud as Fall rewound
At every equinox, again and again.

And when you think of me remember when
I last said Sorry. As the autumns pass
At quarter to five, the time goes fast, and the grass
Will slow its growth. But I am huge in your head,
Pounding. And we're the same. Your blood I've bled.
You're sleeping in my bed now with my bees.
I'm swimming in the hollow sound of seas.

And now I'm swimming in that sound of seas,
The inexhaustible murmur. Now I'm back
To letters at this desk of letters, keys,
Paper and screen, your egomaniac,

Dear critics. The narcissist's tried "art" inside
This paper's looking-glass, distorted, wide
With me and my burned hair, a blistered ember
From the core of the stove's hot comb. And I remember

My silence sweet as canopy beds or a girl
In spinning duchess satin's whispered whirl.
Then, all the days ahead were bees in the attic,
The moments still unseen but heard, ecstatic,

Promising blood as I stood, now stand, all poise,
As if I'll move enough to make a noise.

ANTHONY DEATON

After Troy

Not quite putting on what little power or knowledge
pigeons lay claim to, she nonetheless bids them come.
Launched off cornices,

cathedral arches, they glide
through the gelid air in loose spirals, filling the square.
Their wings beat a thin flat thunder.

She's drifted in from the soot-marbled
housing blocks piled across the Vistula,
making her tramline pilgrimage among the other pensioners

who haunt the Old Town's benches.
Strewn about her feet are crumbled bits of bread crust
and each cupped palm she extends offers more.

The birds pullulate around her ankles,
roost on her shoulders. Aloof from the others,
one fatted pigeon mounts the faded

purple beret she wears against the late October freeze.
This is when I steal the photo.
All day I've kept the camera hidden inside an overcoat pocket,

afraid reducing Warsaw's rebuilt bell towers
and cobblestone vistas to thirty-six frames per roll
would give me away as something I can't help

not wanting to be. Yet I cannot resist the old lady
capped and gowned, as she is, in feather.
She lifts her arms to either side. The unmindful pigeons crowd,

peck along her flightless limbs, mocking her gravity
as they alternately spread and fold their wings.
Or maybe it isn't mockery, but a mutual love that keeps them

flapping there and holds the woman still,
engenders in that coupling a dream of union,
where one light step might shift their weight to sky.

The Refusal

The child asked for money and I gave him nothing.
At the South Africa-Zimbabwe border
I thumbed for a ride. A small boy of maybe
nine or ten asked for money but I gave him nothing.

Try to imagine the heat, and still so early in the day.
At a distance, under the shade of an acacia,
a group of young Zims watched their friend,
small for his age, walk over to me. He wanted money,

extended an empty hand and I gave him nothing.
I gave him nothing. He was young and wore no shoes.
But there was no hesitation in his step; not even the suncooked
pavement fazed him. In the shade his fellows waited

with cool gazes. They needed money too, I was sure.
He wore no shoes. Only a pair of blue slacks
cut off above the knee, a white shirt,
yellowed twine tied round his wrist.

He was young, wore no shoes, and wanted
a little money. Dollars, pula, rand. His friends
watched patiently in the shade. The heat
bore down on the withered scrub dotting the plains

as if to prove there is no limit to ruin. I studied the face
of my pocket watch and glanced into South Africa
for oncoming traffic. The boy with no shoes stood
reflectively at my side, studying me, turning

back to the acacia's shade. Dollars, pula, rand, he said.
He chatted a while, asked if I were English.
His English was poor; the sentences stumbled
over their own inversions. I waited in silence.

The young boys under the tree waited in silence.
The occasional passing car never slowed. And the boy
in blue shorts, white T-shirt, with terrible grammar and no shoes,
ran through his well-rehearsed lines. Dollars, or rand, or pula.

When he left, he tried to make me feel ashamed.
He wanted to say I was making him suffer. He wore no shoes,
his English was minimal: *You are suffering me.*
You are suffering me, he said, when I gave him nothing.

Homeward, Angel

Blasphemy? I'll dare that too, or something like it.
Saint Sebastian, for instance, begging more even after
the archers' quivers hung empty, and him not dead
    and that not grace enough

but he must crawl back for the cudgels'
blunt killing weight, to lay finally brained in a ditch.
He lived badly and died worse.
    A body's persistence – if not body

then soul, or will, or uninterrupted
conductors of kinetic energy – is a sign to behold, a piety.
Conversion? Yes: plaster, canvas, chapels, museums,
    tacked on street corners in Florence,

he poses teetering on heaven's lip, backlit in the wan
yellow nimbus of paradise and martyrdom.
I've passed him countless times without contrition.
    For instance, just as I pass

the porch light left on like an early promise of safe return,
a beacon, a bright belief – now the sulfurous smudge
glowers, now the porch light reproaches this dawn return
    and last night's stretch from beer-hall

to bedroom. Shirt stains, a woman's flavor matted in my beard
are the sweet loose change I carry by the pocketful.
Quiet hall and stairs, give up your sleep and groan
    beneath my homecoming, beneath the felt-muffled

break of pool balls I bring and foot-falls climbing.
What waits with wings for me here?
The neighbors' laundry forgotten on the line
    must try again; that is, the fresh sheets

hang limp with dew; that is, they hold no wind,
nor rise like angels. This morning, birds drop from trees,
the sky drains to the blue lawn. Blasphemy? Fine.
    But for now, say what you will,

I am the sole ascending thing.

MATT DONOVAN

Prelude for Musical Glasses

Something like Melville's honey-hunter leaning in too far,
dying encased in sweetness. Yet without the elegiac whiff.
    Or those songs of Orpheus before the glance back,
when his lyre's strummed guts still made the brambles sag

    with ripe-oozy berries & rivers buck from silt-churning paths
where wild beasts lolled glassy-eyed, inhaling the sugary tunes
    about a bite of tongue-spun apple in Eurydice's mouth
& not much else beyond the sputtering torches & gilded things

    he knew would adorn his wedding day, which would be soon.
Such were the heavenly sounds Ben Franklin made
    as his fingertips skimmed soda-lime bowls rigged to turn
on an iron rod & ever-wet with the rainwater they grazed,

    the rims giving off a ravishing, high-pitched keen that swelled
into the indescribable, never-needing-to-be-tuned sublime.
    Or at least this is more or less how, during the short-lived
glass harp fad, its notes were described as *perfect*. *Armonica*,

    Franklin called it, from the Italian for *harmony*, & for all
his doohickey dabbling – soothing wind-pummeled waves
    with tumblers of oil, that iconic kite lashed by blustering skies –
nothing made him giddier than this contraption he built

    in order to have the unworldly music of angels at the whim
of nearly motionless hands. An instrument he played shuttered tight
    in his cobalt third-floor room, keeping the sun's blare
from each damp spinning glass, the same way he taught

    Marie Antoinette in the velvet-curtained parlors of Versailles
as she stood bejeweled in her diamond-dusted two-foot pouf,
    fingering crystal goblets for the gathered palace crowd
obliged to think of nothing but the tremulous aria she made.

    For hours, they listened, pretending it was all that mattered,
& at times it almost was, as if each piercing note were prelude
    to nothing, severed from any thought of what's to come.
The way, the first time her husband plays, Franklin's wife,

    dragged up from a sheet-thrashing sleep, sits rapt
watching dust motes pour down in a tiny square of light,
    knowing for a moment she's dead. As motionless
as you in a heat-haze at the pier, clutching what's left

    of your fist-warmed coins, listening to a man cram the air
with ethereal noise that is the theme to *Popeye*, that might be
    the worst thing ever made, with his hands fluttering – emphatic,
precise – above the gleaming rows of glasses & where do you go

    from this empty rapture, stock-still, dazzled despite it all?

Exit, Pursued by a Bear

Given the flecks of October stars, the withered scribble
of garden shapes, I sit listening hard to the night as if
there were nothing else to do. Bit of wind & that

on-the-prowl screech-yip of coyotes, something snuffling
the oaks again. Must we love this? Yet another autumn
tramping it down, all the meager stuff we blunder towards,

hoard for consolation, how each day lurches us towards,
as *The Winter's Tale* has it, things dying, things newborn.
If that play is true, someone once began, though I can't imagine

how he finished the thought. Small hope, in any case,
since it's all a fabulous lie: that concocted Bohemian coast,
the long dead resurrected as statue, stepping down

stage-right. And Antigonus eaten by that matter-of-fact bear
after he abandons the child. No one can explain how,
in the months before my son was born, there was a funeral

almost every week. Believe me: since I can't say anything
that seems true about either the dying or newborn, I wish
the detritus from that time might somehow be worth more:

stacks of creamers on red-eye flights, another thick-striped tie.
Or deep within a room that seemed to be lumbering away,
where no one spoke of morphine drips or cancer consuming

a face, a third cousin describing the sky opening in sorrow
after a Longhorn loss. The skies open as Antigonus is mauled
off-stage & the storm swallows a boatload of men

like raisins in flaming brandy – that it's all untrue brings
no one back & between the sea, the wind, the bear & the man,
there's too much roaring to speak of, although a shepherd tries.

He tries even as the howling reaches its pitch, yet exits
whooping of luck since by then he's found the impossible
girl with her basket of gold. Meaning even if there's more

to say about devouring, leave room for blessing, grace.
Thus lying in bed, black clothes crimped on hotel chair-backs
for the next unending day, pressing the rim of a glass

into the unlikely globe of my wife's eight-month belly,
inscribing fast-fading ring upon ring & hearing nothing
of course but at least knowing what I was listening for.

On the Wheel Constructed for the 400th Anniversary of Columbus in the New World

Chicago World's Fair, 1893

built to dwarf   Eiffel's bric-a-brac eyesore   but also to honor
the man who believed   in a pear-shaped world   where seas buckled
towards heaven,   where   throat-swelling frigates   hovered
midair, rudders sliced   yolk-colored weeds & that   one blue-flame streak

cleaved the horizon   as it plummeted   into blackness they knew
would be worlds   of only more waves   before they reached someplace
flat & green,   the most fragrant thing   he would possess, years
from those parrot flocks   blotting out the sun   & all the men, he wrote,

you could make   *do what you wished*,   a wheel was shaped for the man
& this Eden   he thought was a stone's throw   from the Great Khan's
cinnamon, pearls,   even while anchored   in a Haitian lagoon
listening to *bird-song   so marvelous, a man   would never want to leave*

& never did, in praise   of that first glimpse   of land, a far-off speck
that was like   *a little wax candle   bobbing up & down*, Ferris made
a spinning pillar,   a galaxy of lights   with thousands of Edison's
incandescent bulbs   mounted on metal,   *a kind of Ezekial's Wheel*,

he wrote, *a monster*   or what was promised   by one *Guide to the Fair:*
a Tower of Babel   on Lake Michigan's shores,   forged for America,
a cobweb of steel,   the skyline inscribed   with ring upon ring,
bearing plates & struts,   bolts & shafts,   the improbable axle,

arcs & spires lifting you   above the city adrift   just a few years
      before
in a sea of fire   blamed on O'Leary's cow   when swarms of embers
seemed to devour   the world & anything   once hammered, held,
when glass melted   from blocks away   & horses crumpled into
      cinders

as men aimed pistols   into walls of flame,   unsure what else to do,
when nothing could be seen   but fire, whereas now   you could
      see it all:
for fifty cents,   for twenty minutes, falling   first skyward, spinning
in orbit   in a crowd-packed room   moving nowhere & rising still

above the fair's pure-white   made to look like marble,   made to
      gleam
beneath this revolving steel,   above the many-ton cheese   encased
      in iron,
axe-flinging Samoans   bored in their huts,   above Hagenbach's
      bears
in a William Tell routine   & a tiger balanced   on a whip-spun globe,

above *the authentic   Street in Cairo* & reindeers   smothered in
      mid-west heat
near the *largest conveyor belt   in the world*, shuddering,   lurching
      along,
above the half-built failure   that will never be   the Spectatorium
with its never-staged   World Finder show: a Santa Maria modeled
      to scale,

pummeled by waves,   drenched by actual light   that falls even now
on the White City   & Chicago too as the wheel   lifts you above
      the shards
of Plymouth rock,   Kilauea's pyrotechnic   lava-frothing pit,
above Sitting Bull's   bullet-pocked cabin   & the world's only
      building

which could *enclose*   *the Russian army*   but holds instead a
    pageant
of wonders in rows: coats-of-arms, plumbing   & furs, all of
    Shakespeare
lustrous on a vase,   & even if, in a few years,   the wheel will be
crumpled by dynamite   & sold for scrap   after typhoid grips Ferris

a few cities away   where his ashes are held   until the cremator
    is paid,
the wheel spins for now   & you've begun   the descent, falling
    back
towards orchids & hookahs   & Bach's clavichord,   Liberty Bells
    made
from grapefruit, wheat,   & the real Liberty Bel   on loan, under
    guard,

& you can see almost all   of the lead-colored lake   where the
    remade
Nina & Pinta sway   after retracing the path from Spain, circling
    up
to these harbor waves   where they stir, anchored   near the convent
rebuilt brick by brick   to resemble what Columbus   sailed past
    on his way

to find nutmeg, gold,   oceans of silk,   when he heard hymns
of morning prayer,   the same songs,   the *Guide* claims, if you
    listened
you could almost hear too   as you fall   in the glassed-in room
reeling down   *Star of light having risen   Now & forevermore*

MOLLY FISK

Prayer for Joe's Taco Lounge, Mill Valley

Fig-sized red and orange all-year Christmas bulbs
splash their holy light on the plastic-coated tablecloths
and glint against the bottled throats of every brand

of hot sauce – El Yucateco, Tapatio, Doña Maria's –
Mole, singing their fiery songs on a shelf that lines the room,
nestled among a hundred ceramic Madonnas –

Tamazula, Cholula and Crystal beside the beatific
faces of the Mother of us all – and still lives of hard
plastic fruit not invented in this country, not even

in the '40s, and so many crosses, empty and occupied,
paintings of Jesus and the Lord. O, Bufalo,
Valentina, Tabasco, Habañero, guard the bas-relief

bull's head glowering out of its red velvet frame, bless
the photograph of somebody's mother, and the bluefin
tuna leaping on the wall, river of traffic flowing

past the plate glass, sanctify each hot tortilla,
each yellow plastic basket lined with greasy paper,
watch over the customers tonight as they bend

their heads to quesadillas and burritos, Del Fuerte,
if you are listening, carry us safely into tomorrow,
we will praise you by the artificial light of every

electrified tabletop candle, O gods of the spoon-shaped,
the smooth-skinned, searing chiles, comfort us –
keep us warm.

Rowing, November

The way the body wants to pull its own weight,
    hands curled around the shaft of the oar, drawing it clean

through bitter water as blood rushes out the doors
    of your capable heart and cold air billows into both lungs,

the release a kind of violence, oar's brief rest
    as it's feathered, skimming on air and then the quick

turn, the catch, and it grips its width of river again,
    the body in love with use, flat back muscles tight over

shoulder blades, all the bones of the wrist steady, your arms
    pulling hard and straight, fingers curved loose but ready

to grip if the oar hits a pocket of air or a branch,
    submerged, if it scoops a rat's sodden carcass up to the surface

as you pass. You unclench your teeth but set the jaw
    in concentration. The plates of kneecap slide across their ends

of bone as the big thigh muscles contract, relax,
    begin to shake with joy, doing their work. Frost glazes

the drooping willows. Black-crowned herons
    rustle on their secret branches, ready for sleep while your eyes

search now for the first flare of light to smooth
    the curves of the undersides of bridges, sheen of sweat

across your brow, the body's prayer, and steam
    escaping in puffs from your parted lips, hips

balanced an inch over water, the narrow boat
    surging and gliding into another winter.

Pantoum Without Hope of Rescue

This time it's both of them,
half-clothed on their own double bed,
mother and father, husband and wife.
If this upsets you, by all means turn away.

Half-clothed on their own double bed,
their daughter naked between them.
If this upsets you, by all means turn away:
look at the expensive view of the Golden Gate.

Their daughter, naked between them,
used to being invisible flesh.
Look at the expensive view of the Golden Gate.
Think about justice as an abstraction.

Used to being invisible flesh,
she lies with her shoulders in her mother's lap.
Think about justice as an abstraction –
perhaps you'll never need a witness yourself.

She lies with her shoulders in her mother's lap.
They run their hands across her skin like feathers.
Perhaps you'll never need a witness yourself.
The father pushing his way into her.

They run their hands across her skin like feathers.
He likes to hold her legs up as if it's a game,
her father, pushing his way into her,
grinning and panting, saying how good it will feel.

He likes to hold her legs up as if it's a game,
leaning over the child to kiss his happy wife,
grinning and panting, saying how good it will feel,
palming her breasts, glazed with fine sweat.

Leaning over the child to kiss his happy wife
as if they were alone there,
palming her breasts, glazed with fine sweat.
No one is angry. No one cries.

As if they were alone there,
mother and father, husband and wife.
No one is angry. No one cries,
although this time, it's both of them.

MARTHA GREENWALD

The Last Secretary

This morning, in the ladies room mirror,
She realizes her blouse is message-pad pink.

Her whole torso contains choices waiting
To be checked-off and dispensed with down the hall ...

While You Were Out, sickened by the foul air,
What happened? Three calls, four faxes, then

The computer chimes its happy middle C –
New mail. Another and another chain letter:

"Forward this message ten times to find lost loves,
Twenty, and golden fortune will fly into your lap."

Bad luck befalls those who do not participate.
Remember the legendary examples who declined,

Deleted their letters, then died within weeks –
Miss X from Texas, blackened in a fiery wreck;

Janine H, the beautiful, midwestern receptionist,
Drowned on her honeymoon by a mad gondolier.

Who needs uninvited foreboding stapled to the day,
The dread of going home to what was your home,

When instead, by playing along, the power
Of the unsent might retreat at least until noon.

Downstairs, women leave, wrapped in long wool coats.
My dear, what *did* happen while you were out?

Lunch is crackers, a freeze-dried cup of soup.
The peas and carrots bloom in the boiling water.

Other Prohibited Items

"... try not to over-think these guidelines." – Southwest.com Carry-on Tips

No to his bassoon. No to their cricket bat.
No to your robot, her corkscrew, that hatchet.
Good traveler, whose children might be overjoyed –

Next trip, please procure toys that resemble toys.
Policy does not ban pink princess/pirate swords
But for security, we confiscate all backstories

(Though adaptations are few). Item: one wrench
From a beloved uncle's workbench, pilfered
After his funeral, just before the flight. Lost thanks

For his kindnesses, the raucous Christmas pranks –
Although he taught his nephew the lathe, relinquish
The memento at our checkpoint. Item: rose oil,

Decanted by monks, four ounces in a faceted flacon.
Rare, the passenger whispers, hushed, as if pleading
To the lover for whom the secret gift was intended.

Well, her kiss may *be* sublime but no to the perfume's
Ounce of excess; and no to the antique drawknife,
Despite its moonstone handle, studded with marcasite.

Again, mid-shift, a woman about to board a red-eye
Puts her Ziploc on the x-ray conveyor, then flusters
When we screen the bag's contents. The bottles warm

Our gloved hands. Milk rivulets dampen our sleeves.
However, her infant waits at the destination, so toss
Her bottles to the take-bin, foremilk already separating

From hindmilk. No to her umbrella, unruly & floral.
Sorry – storm phobias never justify hollow finials.
No exceptions for the sentimental or exceptional.

Our take-bins swell with keepsakes decades misplaced,
With longings for the heft of a snowglobe balanced
On a small palm. Look inside – old Snow White

Sleeps in a dubious solution. No to her domed sky's
Blizzard. No to the castle, no to apples. Witches lurk
In these woods, and every poisoned pie is gooseberry.

DANIEL GROVES

A Dog's Life

A stay of execution: one last day,
your day, old Everydog, then, as they say,
or as we say (a new trick to avoid
finalities implicit in destroyed),
you have to be *put down*, or *put to sleep* –
the very dog who always fought to keep
from putting down, despite our shouts, a shoe
before its bottom sole was gnawed straight through;
and sat awake, our sleepless nights, to bark
away some menace looming in the dark.

No picking up the sense of all this talk;
you only prick your ears to hear a *walk*,
or else, the ultimate reward, a *car*? –
My God, tomorrow's ride … Well, here we are,
right now. You stare at me and wag your tail.
I stare back, dog-like: big and dumb. Words fail.
No more commands, ignore my monologue,
go wander off. Good dog. You're a good dog;
and never quite could master, anyway,
the execution, as it were, of *Stay*.

Portrait

I. Aperture

> *The monkey is the only producer of pictures*
> *who imitates nothing ... and recognizes only the*
> *unadulterated pleasure of the disruptive mark*
> – Thierry Lenain, *Monkey Painting*

That old scene – monkey see and monkey do –
is done. That organizing grind, the grid,
is barred. Guerilla movements must exclude
such cagey, simian similitude,
banana republic exhibitions rid
the colony of artists. It's a zoo.

Or New World Order? Pleased to trace our line
from theirs, the prim revere a primitive –
wrenching, illuminating – by Ape X.
Abstract expression climbing toward its apex?
Creation thus evolving to outlive
our monkish copying? A monkeyshine?

We draw on our background (animals instinct
with second nature – God, the strain), that dark
age of which we – continent, prehensile
detailers, great apologists, with stencil
and rule – make light, for this *disruptive mark*,
to miss it, feeling, in the missing, linked.

II. Image

Featuring the complete line of Canon *copiers*
– Advertisement

Outside the window, sheets of rain, the garden;
inside, the earth-toned ceiling sprouts a patch
of sprinklers, all aligned like silver flowers
to spray the cloud-gray tiled floor with showers
(the copier alone may strike a match).
Temps vanish, gone to smoke. I beg their pardon.

Reflecting in a depthless black, I smack
the next original against the glass,
face down, and shut the lid – a blinding light –
its spitting image spits right up, upright.
Dual echoes, out of Catechism class,
reprove me now, my hand laid on the stack:

Salvation in the Information Age?
Or just mass reproduction? This debate
repeats itself, subsides – CLEAR PAPER JAM
(these damn contraptions). I am that I am;
a copy copies, but cannot translate
the space beyond the margins of each page.

Novella

A reedy melody – tripping, banal –
floats upon the incensed, disinfectant
miasma that receives my slow, expectant
constitutional along Canal.

It's catchy – today's Parade of Chariots'
calliopede procession passes by
(waves of Pacific Blue to pacify
the Krishna kids); Ozzie and Harriet's

self-righteous dudes ride out their surfeit, bored;
all *Grecian Formula* and *Tiger Balm*,
a Mexi-Cali thug extends a palm
tree's shadow, while the brazen *Gold's Gym* horde,

in demonstrating monstrous, taut contortions
of muscle (bound, if slightly, by a *Speedo*),
draws sighs along our replicated lido.
A groan to academic disproportions?

Socratic irony? The great unknown
guitarist jams, the cokeheads go coquettish
to music from another fuming fetish –
the belch of Hell's Angelic monotone

convulsing through a buffed-to-mirror chrome
and leather-perfect, idling motorcycle,
evokes a certain choked-up fin-de-siecle
refrain augmented by a reverb *Om*.

Out of the smog (this high, august occasion)
the Santa Monicas appear to bless
the progress – swollen, now; I must confess
a weakness for retro-alien contagion,

its bouquet (vintage 1968),
its public airing (teen-age Dionysian)
in which, in concert with our Dietician/
Gurus, we privately asphyxiate.

Boys will be boys... (this precious sense of pathos,
this blind conviction that – the damnedest thing –
the unlived life is worth examining).
Past "PSYCHIC READINGS: 50 cents (5 pesos),"

the setting sun sets up my parting speech –
Like, later, man (the Valley diction) – said
for guys like Will, or Todd (pure *Bill & Ted*).
I lie in wait for death in Venice Beach.

Balder –

A muffled scream of sheer hot air,
parting gone from scarcely there
by a hair's breadth; a face that grinned
so long in the teeth of comb and wind
grown longer, blown dry, sucking breath –
each morning brings a brush with death;
a reaping with no reparation;
my Calvinist predestination:
Male Pattern Baldness, patterning
a semi-circle, unclosed ring,
almost the perfect symbol of
eternally renewed self-love;
unlucky horseshoe where (where else?)
the "almost" counts, as it repels
all but shavings, and entails
the Omega of the Alpha Male's
bewildering caprice. Magnetic
fields have withered – left ascetic,
barren, not to be reseeded –
and curling, crested waves receded
with the dark abounding mane ...
O Vanity, what will remain?
As, in the fall-out, I – braincase
distressed, unlocked, no hair in place,
no hair accounted for, uncrowned,
uprooted, stranded – cut around
my losses (greater everyday),
what will remain? A hell to pay,
a toupee hell – swept-under rugs,
shameless, self-advertising plugs?
These fragments I have shorn, a ruing
of any 'do as my undoing.
Teasings of time and space – white holes,
big bangs, celestial spheres and polls?
A bounty on my head – sprays, creams,
and overblown comb-over schemes
through which (fool captiousness, the will

o' the wisps) the naked truth shines, still?
Or else, if not hair-triggered pride,
the pater-pated, eagle-eyed
empty-nester's spite – outliving
full-bodied barbarism, giving
hirsute suitors passing by
(so stylish, now) the bald-faced lie.
An ahistorical flip-flop?
Round head or restoration fop?
Rag-top or chrome bumper crop?
Loose clippings or a stapled sheaf?
Security blanket or ... good grief.
O Vanity, the mirror kills
conditioned hope in miracles;
the widow's peak puts none too fine
a point on our ingrown decline;
its caul recalls each blushing bride
to whom we, shock by shock, have died,
on its ascension towards a thick,
blunt prominence – a bone to pick
in martyrdom, where every pelt
(upon the lack of one) is felt
too deeply; a ridge too wide across,
too bare, with too high-brow a gloss;
Place of the Skull ... indeed, too much.
All flesh's coup de grace – light touch
against the temples, whisper-rush
that soothes unto the end, low hush
that softens its own blow – the wind
blows till we listeth, will rescind
us all, O Vanity, will grant,
to our last heir, the sole remnant,
his ever-fashionable wish,
O Vanity – to vanish, vanish.

A Stranger Here

... that benighted city.
– Frank Lloyd Wright

Escaping placement, fleetingly *(...Brick House)*,
funk follows formstone out of vacant blocks;
as row on row of more brick houses drowse
in sprawling shade, the last carthorse click-clocks
in time to when, her ships come in, the docks
were bustling – *swart, side-burned, the common boors
unloaded wares for Clipper commodores...*

Loaded nowheres; the Broadway (too broad, indeed)
of memory, yoking past and present – witty
or cavalier – failing what we succeed
(hard fact, brick factory in complicity
with dream, our unincorporated city,
Retropolis). Though where but this co-here
could all our incoherencies cohere?

Such as the concrete underneath my feet,
and – high abstraction – signs above my head
(downtown and uptown – both a one-way street,
but parallel): ST. PAUL and CHARLES. Misled,
perhaps, by mere book smarts, too many dead
white males, my do-it-yourselfer projects upon
historic structures, fallen, nearly gone,

the will to restoration – which, of course,
entails conversion, also – thus the former
fills a function (cart behind the horse).
That old-line statesman, gentlemanly farmer
Lord Baltimore could not provide for more
than meets the idling idealist today
of Jacobite angel-wrestling, holding sway

through centuries of tension: Druid Hill,
Greek Town; the steadfast *Bromo-Seltzer* tower,
Domino's Sugar; Pig Town, Butcher's Hill;
storefront Baptist churches, 24-hour
Rite-Aid; Beth Steel, LaCrosse; a higher power,
up with *The Sun* clock-punching; rhyme, meter;
Lyric Opera House, Mechanic Theater.

Diversions, horseplay, hackwork: arm in arm,
these couples make a scene that made out worse,
decades "The Monumental" into "Charm"
city quietly declined. Perverse
horror, or pragmatism? Poe and Peirce
died poor, dispersed, as Mencken's burboisie,
(ever-mercurial) sounded-off Key,

with coltish *unitas*, unto the local
heavens (blue horseshoe collar, aureole
of looming lights) for Weaver and, lo, Cal
before they took the field at Memorial
away, and picked its carcass clean. Its soul?
Nevermore? The ravings carry on
(no bardic songbird, only carrion).

To join the lost cause, beat a dead horse,
drink at the Hippo (if not Hippocrene) –
my (equi)vocation, mixing metaphors
for this Metapolis, moving between
READ and CHASE (at EAGER, epicene
epicenter) and backward – significantly? –
since age eighteen, from UNIVERSITY.

My twenties amid the Thirties – classic white
marble stoops to conquer, an attic room.
But thirties amid the Twenties? Forties – wait,
I-40? The Inner Harbor's recovered womb?
Through netherhoods of dome and spire, doom
and aspiration, what prestigial
detail remains of such original

old glories, grandeurs? Charm as monument?
The antiquated anti-quaint? The odd
wrought-iron frontispiece on Space for Rent,
the odd wrought-iron star on the façade,
remember, bears a load (but household god
gargoyles' stone-faced perseverance is
only to keep up disappearances).

Form follows function – will, that is, outlive
its use. Though fretwork, grating, colored pane
and painted screen – fancy, if useless – give
perspective. Elaborate frames that show their strain
(the crack, the pipes); the imminent domain
of fixer-uppers – junk supplies our fix:
the *ton* of bric-a-brac, or the ton of bricks.

Could building blocks that, layer on layer (bored,
martyred, mortar-boarded), we pre-cast to spell,
from TIME and LABOR, BALTIMORE, be floored,
dropping, again, to BLAME and RIOT? Well,
one noticed, visiting, in those who dwell
in this *De trop*olis, "an inverse pride
in not being noticed." Suicide,

like immortality, would draw too much
attention. The *National Bohemian*
natty beau fades out, with no retouch,
winking conspiratorially, man-to-man.
Suspenders, dandy moustache, frothy can –
the trademark properties, condemned, persist
for fetishist and counterfeitishist,

stung with nostalgia by some buzzword ("Hon"),
by beehive sentimentality, sickly sweet,
glazed over, overdone, over and done,
done over. My baroque-ial school aesthete
keeps the faith, invokes the Absolete,
the cataclysm, the holy trivia quiz
"as it was in the beginning, shall be, is,

without end." Greek Revival; Drag Queen Anne;
Flamboyant Gothic; Georgian; French Chateau;
Carthorse; Iron Horse; the Iron Man;
cart blanche; wrought irony; my B & O
roundhouse (its trains of thought, however slow,
linked-up to a one-track mind to run,
always on time, birth to oblivion,

Golden, Gilded, Gelded Ages hence…)
into the turn, the backstretch, comes the night-
mare, my railbird's dark horse, with a sense
of show, and place, and loss, to find daylight
across the bay to which – not yet, not quite –
all are brought (the racing form, the poem,
and I, perfunctorily, follow), head for home.

JAMEY HECHT

Zapruder Film Frame 155

Steady as she goes. This is maybe three feet down
the road from where we were. Excruciating, isn't it?
Nailing him this slowly is barbaric, but that's cinema:
The tiny dark blue car is dust and plastic in my VCR.

New money shoots toward Heaven from a punctured hill.
The algal blooms of 90 million years ago have turned
to bitumen and kerogen and fumes, and now like whiskey
in a still, it's transubstantiated into gold and burned.

Every grain of silver nitrate on this frame of film
once lay undiscovered in the dark below the mine.
The very gasoline was once alive. Those are pearls
that were his shining eyes, and dirt that was his face.

Look: Love is tugging backward on the limousine,
while murder effortlessly moves it into place.

Zapruder Film Frame 197

What comes through me now? These seeds of hell,
the mother's body and the father's word, are planted
in my arteries to stop me and the sound
of many waters folds the centuries to come,

tightly like the flag some military funeral presents
to parents of the fool that left his bed for destiny
and came back rotting in a plastic bag. The sound
of water falling into water, or of wind into wind,

replaces every voice or revving engine or alarm
from someone else inside the car, who's shot
or scared. I am alone now with this ancient sound,
so new to me, that carries home no meaning

only presence, presence and then emptiness.
First my hearing vanishes, and then I follow it.

JAIMEE HILLS

Chlamydia

Verbophobia: Fear of Words

Like *cellar door*,
Chlamydia.
There's melody cloaked in the malady.
Forget the cinderblocks, the grimy ground
behind the words, like the brutality
of the rain. Hear its lovely drum, the sound
Chlamydia
caught in the downpour.

Like clematis,
Chlamydia,
a clitoris by any other name.
The name as sweet might mean a creeping flower,
petal-clad, wearing the silky plume
of traveler's joy, snowdrift, virgin's bower,
chlamydia,
or sating curls.

Like Clytemnestra,
Chlamydia
(whose mother Leda caught it from a swan).
It ought to be the color tangerine,
a lightning storm, a high-class salon,
this parasite who should have been a queen,
Chlamydia,
another Cleopatra.

Like Fragonard,
Chlamydia.
In a French Rococo garden, light and gaudy,
it drapes a woman on a swing mid-swoop
as a man kneels below her skirt – both bawdy

in their powdered wigs, her pose, his gape.
Chlamydia
should swap with *fulgid*.

Nothing Rhymes with Gitmo

Optophobia: Fear of Opening One's Eyes

The monoglot might slip on *guano-*
toh-moh. You tell dogs *git*, and gung-ho
handy types'll get her done.
Git mo' for less. As slick as a Ginsu
we nick up names and butcher lingo.
The foreign sounds familiar, Gringo.

It's our pet name, a Geico gecko
or a Tamagachi gizmo,
our little pal, the tickle-me-Gitmo,
as common as your local Citgo.
We quickly fill the Winnebago
and sort the *Logos* from the logo.

A nimble moniker suited FloJo,
her name and legs, a quick glissando.
Consider celebrity: our Hojo,
J-Lo, Brangelina, Brando –
abstract concepts, magnificos.
Much to grand, their names are name-brands.

Consider the word *snafu*, like Garbo,
delicate, posh, a slight *faux pas*.
The war-born acrimony, acro-
nymed, gets lost to sound bite, footnote,
shortcut, whatnot. Charlie, Pinko,
Jerry. Consider how the Gingko

tree, botanical dynamo,
survived a bombed Hiroshima.
A hail of syllables can hit
like bullets on Geronimo.
Language survives this way. Now,
enunciate. *Guantánamo*.

JAIMEE HILLS

KAREN HOLMBERG

Imago

Io Moth

Because it confined us
outside its patent-slick capsule,
because no mortal eye can bear
witness to change gradual
as it is wondrous, we lost interest in
the miracle on our sill.
How long ago the burgundy hooks
embedded their stitches in the laurel leaf
is anyone's guess. That lean-to's
gone auburn, propped weeks ago
inside the sheer-walled oubliette.
We pet the forehead, high-domed
as a day-old kitten's. The antennae
shiver so exquisitely we expect the vanes,
mimosa-like, to fold. Nudging our finger
along the edge of the wing
tautens the abdomen to the leaf. Tightens
the tongue's coil to a tiny coin
in the plush breast.
Pearlescent minerals
come off on our fingers.
The forewings swag like curtains
above a stage. We absorb the set design:
out a hollow like the mouth
on a mask of tragedy
an owl gazes, pupils banded
in bullion gold. And in the absolute black
of each telescope field, a chalky light
lifts into relief the coarse cheek
of an old, flawed pearl,
the dwindling memento of our world.
Our hair stirs in the silent draft
of wings. As if it is Clio, muse of history,

launching from the throat of the noble oak,
never to return,
never to tell us how she fit
all those tapestries and ancient maps
in such a small scroll.

Man o' War

Sunk to the chin in warm
inlet waters, some instinct nudged
    and I turned to see the harbinger
        of on-shore winds: the man o' war
        lightly cantering over
    the tide ripples' peaks.

Through its skin, puckered
as blown glass, the bright towels, neon
    buckets and shovels
        warped and bulged,
        violet hued:
    a world viewed
  through the legs streaking
    a wine glass.

Even then I sensed
a sexuality, labial and testicular;
    silky, sticky, stinging below surface
        as the net of nerves and clotted tentacles
        sieved the water,
    the viscous ropes furred
  with millions of hair-trigger harpoons
    tattooing their prey with venom lethal
as a cobra's.

By morning, turgid sacs
in thousands trailed pennants surf-torn,
    tumbled to ribbons, eliciting
        that particular pity
        when the treacherous
    goes slack, turns
  ludicrous in fact, sand grains
    clinging to gelatin
flesh like sugar candying fruit.

And still it would subtly
wince and shrink, tempting me
    to pinch the float
        between thumb and finger
        and fling those welting reins
    to the draining wave.

When I was four or five I watched
my grandfather – Head of Lifeguards, still
    a muscleman – bend a woman back
        in thigh deep water,
        his gloved fingers
    peeling tentacles that wound
her neck in yards
    of rotted silk.

How gently he untangled
that shawl, knowing
    each fragment he broke off
        could generate a new individual,
        could arrow forth
    into the surf
soft spurts of poison.

LESLEY JENIKE

Against Ornamentation

That one does not inlay every coffee table
with mother of pearl! Covering wood
with the stuff of the sea denies division.

Even here, in the tiniest room, I'm apart
from you. So is braided bullion apart
from its curtain, egg tempera from the hen.

Filigreed into every door are the names
of persons compelled to, by etching, redo
trees now bent under their carved shorthand,

a tendency to spangle every space with angel
or cloud, as if sky's not enough or face:
a joining of two planes, either side the ocean.

A Rauschenberg Conversation

"The artist's job is to be a witness to his time in history."
– Robert Rauschenberg

He asked me about the painting that's black. Just black.
    And wondered if its blackness is somehow representative

of the twenty-first century dead, dead because we had
    every opportunity and blew every opportunity and I sd,

No. This was painted during the twentieth and so reflects
    an apocalyptic return to what's original and what's more

original? No. I see possibility in futures that will contain
    the hum of a breathing machine carried in an easy breeze

through a window just to catch in the arms of a potted tree.
    This is the twenty-first century. Encoded in the DNA

of every living thing is a sketch of the man or woman
    that will bear witness to your demise, my demise,

the demise of a pet that in sleep twitches in an incalculable
    pet dream world and all the while Florida will grow more

Florida with its sun, prehistoric mid-section sprouting
    embarrassingly thick, dark hair where hair should never

grow. And I reminded him: Below the black is a strip
    of news and the news, I guess, never ends even after

history has etched its loss and its gain into recusant
    material, I mean recyclable. In the middle of the gallery

he just looked at me, at the painting, back at me
    and sd, Where is the human figure? What happened

   to the figure who in terrible gesture remakes the air
        around him? Isn't he both the blackness and the news

and isn't he, asleep in amnion, even then, before birth
        and after stellar reconnaissance, the textbook definition,

the end and the all that *is* and *was* – no god , no fall?

Self-Portrait as the Golden Head at Jardin de Luxembourg

The corrupt incorrigible with heavy bags swing,
prone to kisses from boys in black shirts
and horn-rimmed glasses, through the garden,

some in packs, some alone with their tobacco,
dying for another glass of wine or day's first,
while bodiless Head stares golden from its shackle

above a rut of dirt. Minus torso, heart's tender
lacks a hiding place, so moves beyond the usual
clenched fist or apple core – what we remember

the heart to be – and spills in every direction,
as shadows spill across a gazing pool and rising
immaculate Head watches lidless, affection

for its lack darkening path that leads
down rows and rows of trunkless trees.

A Rothko Conversation

"We favor the simple expression of the complex thought. We are for the large shape because it has the impact of the unequivocal. We wish to reassert the picture plane. We are for flat forms because they destroy illusion and reveal truth."
– Rothko

He had a ticket to an all-age show. Is that, you asked, an excuse? No.
To end one's life is to force matters to a conclusion the universe
wouldn't agree to – utterly American in his rapacity despite the
    subtle

streaks of color. The cool, waiting folds of a feather bed are graves
in another country, dug to clasp bodies we didn't know or forgot
in an earthy embrace this painter calls bleeding – a pint of oneself

escapes while the rest, diminished, keeps flowing. Arteries of streets
and country paths, no matter, all lead to one heart and that is, you
    sd,
the core. No more. No less. Your brand of religiosity, I sd, is a mess.

What of the scattered bleeping smears on a windshield after you've
driven through? As far as I know, dead no matter the species don't
join to make one mighty band of color but rather stay as they are:

dead. Or the wild boar I saw once strapped to the hood of a car: no
dignity. Or the woman at the piano who imagines her song goes out
to everyone only hits the walls of her bedroom – a splotch of sound

floating for a moment above the others (a cry, a punch), before it
dissolves into adieu. And that, I sd, is what this particular artist
is trying to do: Show how trembling, sad and separate we are. But,

you sd, We share a common surface. Fine. That's true. Still,
the canvas kills our precious little claims on life with size,
huge in appetite – a triumphant and unrepentant American will.

CARRIE JERRELL

The Poet Prays to Her Radio for a Country Song

O guardian of the well-lunged, purveyor of lies,
enabler of the backseat horny, I am sorely afflicted.
Traveling the long tongue of highway 40,
I fear the bottomless black sky of loneliness
has hawked me from the back of its throat
and doomed me to land, wet and without notice,
in the dust-bitten spittoon of Oklahoma.

Have mercy, and do not leave me in my despair
to the size two pop star's manufactured vibrato
or my own heavy static. I confess I drive
a foreign make. I refuse to use home color
on my hair, and once again I've let heartbreak
put his hands in my back pockets. How I need
a song tonight – the kind that's all curves,
that's two parts sex and one part scripture,
that wears work boots to wardrobe
on opening night and when handed pink chiffon
says, *Baby, you know I don't do delicate*.

Descend, you blue jean honky-tonk angels,
and play my pain in 4/4 time on fiddle and red
birdseye-aproned steel guitar. Let my voice be open
as a screen door, all latchless and breeze-blown,
all invitation. May it reach like a revival choir
my man standing by the entrance, and may he tug
at his collar from the heat. Minor spirit,
I have been blinded by love's late night hallelujahs,
but I hear the blue notes coming. I've had enough
measures of introduction. Let me testify.

The Country-Western Singer's Ex-Wife, Sober in Mendocino County, California

Somewhere back East my late love's all coked up,
another cowgirl wannabe lying
at his feet while he plucks a Willie Nelson song
from his beer-soaked six string and complains nobody
understands a rebel's broken heart.
I've played her part, the starstruck blonde in boots

and denim mini, boobs and brains to boot.
Whiskey-fed, dreamy, how I talked him up,
a sequined Tammy to his George, my heart
a backstage bed I wanted him to lie in.
It proved too hard, and when a harder body
came along, he said, *The party's over*,

and left me listening to "Sad Songs and Waltzes,"
Waylon, steel guitars that struck like a boot
to the face. But that's good country, right? A body
enamored with its bruises, praising its screw-ups,
the blood still wet in its wounds? Memory lies
as still as a rattlesnake until my heart

begs for its venom. *Sink 'em in,* my heart
says. *I've been traveling on a horse called Music,
and he's brought me here to die.* I'd be lying
if I said I didn't want to fill my ex's boots
with spit the night I caught him with that up-
start starlet at the bar; when everybody

tried to hide in their shot glasses; when nobody
but a Broadway street preacher had the heart
to hold my hair off my face while I threw up
outside; when all the songs I loved – "Crazy,"
"Golden Ring," "Jolene" – became like boots
too busted to put on, bent-pitch ballads of his lies,

my shame sung loud in the key of C. He's lying
from the stage, in the bar or bed, when he says nobody
understands him. I do. I've burned my boots,
moved west to wine and water because his heart
was a dry bottle, cold as the black rose
rotting in his lapel, and I still wake up

to his tunes: the beer, blow, boots and love, the lies
they tell and don't. Once, I was a good-hearted woman.
Now I pray, Lord, please, somebody, shut him up.

The Poet Prays to the 9mm under the Driver's Seat

Coldest friend, pretty little monster,
I know relief lies low and left of center.

I'm looking for it now. The windshield
shines with my body's outline on its field

of nighttime glass, of stars on glass, though I'm
no star, just a waning mark at which to aim

my crooked sights. My days are all dry-fires,
and better actions call for calibers higher

than my own. Be savior to my lovesick bones,
groom to the primed bride of my loneliness,

and I'll forever be your best brief muse,
your straightest shooter. You have a way with wounds,

with damage and deliverance, and I make
a ready berm for both. Let your trigger's break

perform my lullaby. I'll hold the final note.
Bury it here, in the hollow of my throat.

The Bridesmaid

Having played the roles of bride's best friend, groom's sister,
last minute fill-in, and token female cousin,
you're set for dyed-to-match high heels, the blister,
cold beef, warm beer, the chicken dance, and the dozen

well-meaning guests who pat your hand and ask,
Have you found someone special yet, sweetheart?
You've learned to include in the day's costume a mask,
a practiced smile and sigh to check your smart-

ass answer: what you've found are bantamweight
boy toys, e-freaks, sex pervs, and two prospects
who might have worked, had they not been mean or married.

What's special is the bubble bath that waits
at home, where a worn-out welcome mat bedecks
the threshold over which you won't be carried.

The Best Man

Spring Break with your Sig Ep brothers means blackjack
at Mirage, the Tropicana's topless show,
flaming cocktails at VooDoo Lounge, then back
to sleep it off poolside at Bellagio,

until one *frater*, Clooney-style, hooks up
with a Harrah's hostess – tattoo, belly ring,
implants, the works – and, oh, he's all shook up,
pawning his pledge pin for back alley bling

and dragging you to chapel, where he and his wait, er,
wife-to-be exchange their vows before God,
Elvis, and a stoned Priscilla impersonator.

You slap your brother's ass, get drunk, applaud
his moves, and turn a glazed eye to his mess
(just like old times), which is what you do best.

The Maid of Honor

As leader of your best friend's satin posse,
your duties include pre-photo makeup checks,
guarding the gifts, preventing the Triple-sec-
soaked in-laws from doing a risqué Bob Fosse

number on the table tops – a job
akin to that of foiling evil spirits,
like Roman maids first had. Here, evil rears its
ugly head in many ways: the poor slob

hoarding the hors d'oeuvres, the screaming kids,
and even, when your friend shows up months later
with a suitcase and a boutonnière-size bruise,

the groom. She's stunned, in danger, trapped on the skids,
and you're still playing the hero, the Mitigator,
a shield from trouble she does and does not choose.

When the Rider is Hope

We pilot evening's cryptic air
fused as faith and plea in prayer.
My burden's to become pure flight;
his, to right me if I scare.

When my blind spot blurs the fence,
he imparts his confidence:
his *Easy girl,* his loose-rein hands,
reprimand my reticence.

Heel to rib, approach then thrust,
I'm suspended by his trust,
playing earth's brief renegade
in bascules made of breath and dust.

I Am Thinking of My First Horse

after Teresa Ballard

A dun, his body the only kingdom
I know the whole of. His cheek broader
than the shoulder blade he rubs it against,
my shoulder blade. I braid his hair
like my hair: mine, the color of sweet feed;
his, night river black. I bathe his saddle marks,
cinch marks, bridle sores, though I cannot
give him back his body unbroken,
the way I have been promised mine
in heaven. Because each morning the world
nuzzles me awake; because my breath
and sunlight and the wind-lashed shadows
of branches outside my window form
a tangled braid of tributaries I will one day
ride to a river dark as a horse's eye;
because I imagine he waits on the bank
to carry me, I am thinking of my first horse,
how we will leave our scars in the water
behind us, entering a kingdom we praise
but cannot ever fully know.
I am thinking of my first horse
because I want no heaven without him.

After the Revival

We gather at the river in our polyester blends.
We gather in our sunburnt skins,
sore from the daylong sermon, a bright
congregation of frailties. To my right,
a man cleans his trifocals with his shirtfront.
To my left, a woman taps her titanium knee,
says, *It'll outlast me*. From weed
and willow edging the bank, the vellum
whir of yellowjackets stirs my hand
to touch three scars from childhood stings
along my jaw, three scars from the day
of my baptism, three stings as I stood
by the river, my throat swelling and swelling
until I dropped to my knees in the clearing,
my hair still wet when my father at last laid
one hand on my shoulder, prayed,
Spare my daughter, then jammed the EpiPen
into my thigh. By which I was saved,
the plea or the needle, I can't say,
but before breath rattled its wings
behind my teeth again, I witnessed
the bunched velvet of thunderclouds
drag the distant ridgeline like a robe's
soiled trim across nails. My own Sinai,
my burning bush, I should have prophesied
but couldn't, too numb, unsure, and only twelve,
though the elders stood with their amens
poised around me. Since then, my throat's
been numbed by different means: horrors of love;
horrors of doubt; a sister's child laid to rest
in a wet grave; my father's stumbling
over stones in the fields he's plowed,
two black spots blooming in each of his eyes.
I've trusted too often the lens doctored
in chemical heat and not the eyes behind
my eyes, but this evening, after new humbling
and hymns tendered by failed voices, I see

that each willow leaf backlit by the apricot sun
is actually a candle set aglow and hovering.
My father stands there in invisible water,
blessing the baptized, his hands reading
their faces, and the air around him is quick
with thousands of wings. O Death,
so proud in your jacket of cheeriest yellow,
this world is a dark cloak I tire of wearing.
Take my eyes and hands. Take my throat
and the songs it traps, and I will still
remember those promises made in the shapes
of rivers. I am waiting for you here
on bended knees. Do not hide from me now.

When the Rider is Truth

I am froth and lather, sent steaming
through jade fields while he sits
heavy in the saddle, beating love songs
on my flanks I'm slow to learn.
His snapped whip rings like church bells.
He prays my name. In different winds,
it rhymes with *win* and *race*. At night,
he rests against my neck and tells me
stars are born between my heartbeats,
though they're unreachable this trip.
Still, with him I feel sure-footed
running on this soil of sand,
this miraculous green,
where every day is like no other
in its symmetry of hill and valley.
When shadows blend, I want the blinders on.
I want the spurs and speed. It's then
I understand tight reins, the firm grip,
the bitter iron on my tongue,
the blood and sharper bit I'm driven with.

ROSE KELLEHER

Ditty

The saddest songs are those that drip
like sweat down the sides of a lemonade pitcher.
Sing me a drink about money gone missing,
serve it up tart with a hillbilly twist:
the bitterer the better, to make the mouth pucker
and gather up the slack.

The saddest songs are those that burn
black as a match and a bundle o' tinder.
Kindle a ditty on daddy gone drifting,
wind it around with a pennywhistle riff;
slowly unroll each note, dark
as smoke from a chimney stack.

The saddest songs are those that fade
like footprints over Siberian tundra.
Shiver the strings of a welcome winter,
shovel it under, drumbeat deep;
naked and bleak as the trees of Tunguska,
laid out back to back.

Asperger's Muse

Once again he's chanting in
a metronomic monotone
the numbers that he's memorized
without a pause for inhalation,
back and forth, a reassuring
rhythm. He has sung his favorite
song so often I should know it:
3.141592
65358979
32384626;
that's as much as I remember.
He, however, keeps on going,
eyes averted, elbows held
as if by magnets to his ribs.
He does it when he's nervous. If
you try to interrupt him, that
will only make him sing it louder.
43383279
50288419
71693993;
Seeking spoken sanctuary
in the perfect circle's key,
he draws a closed perimeter
around himself; and though I cannot
understand the tongue he speaks,
I know he sings a hymn to something
steady, central, infinite.

Zeitoun

What if you were, as I suspect,
a hologram,
a Coptic tourist trap, a scam
the mortal eye could not detect?

What if photons, fiddled with,
beguiled the eye,
glittering in the Cairo sky,
a brilliant flimflam veiled in myth?

What if the world, wanting a mother,
embraced a ruse,
thousands of Muslims, Christians, Jews,
fooled into seeing the light together?

And what if the only light to see
is in the faces
of foolish crowds in sacred places?
Our Lady of Light, enlighten me.

Neanderthal Bone Flute

Let it be a flute. Let some young man,
perhaps red-haired, have carved it just for fun.
Or better yet, to serenade someone:
one of the jut-chinned girls, not of his clan,
a stranger from the east. And let his genes
thrive still in solitary types, the shy
who fidget when you look them in the eye,
the tongue-tied, who must woo by other means.

Ignore the new genetic tests that say
the girl rejected him, that winter came
and spear could not compete with bow and arrow;
that want, or slaughter, whittled him away
because his ways and ours were not the same.
Let bone be flute, the music in our marrow.

Impulse

By thinking – up, back, swivel to the right –
a Rhesus brain controls a robot's arm
over a wireless channel; while tonight
you keep me warm

under the covers with your fevered skin,
hairy as any ape. In either case
an impulse jumps a synapse; dreams begin
to take up space

in ways that bodies do. The high-pitched whine
of monkey-driven metal switching gears,
the interlocking of your legs with mine,
are just ideas

telegraphed into things: thoughts that stray
from gray matter to motor, leaving grooves
of memory that run whichever way
the spirit moves.

Noted Sadomasochists

Jean-Jacques Rousseau

Impossible, unnatural; a knight
can't ask for that. No blushing heroine
could love a stooping, groveling Gawain.
Mon Dieu! She'd shriek with laughter at the sight,

summoning all her maids, who'd point and taunt,
and tell the world your secret. In her eyes
you'd be grotesque, a clown with a disease.
Some things it's just ridiculous to want.

To go on wanting hurts a little less
at any given moment, a slow flame
under the spit you'll die on, in due time.
So hush. It would be madness to confess.

Algernon Swinburne

In the heart of Hermaphroditus,
    Where the hawk is at one with the dove,
Contradictions that shock and delight us
    Are joined in a curious love.
In the virtuous mouth of a devil,
    A curse and a kiss are the same,
So an innocent sinner may revel
    In glorious shame.

In the brilliance of gold that is beaten,
    In the wrath of a merciful god,
In the noble traditions of Eton,
    In the serpent that rose from the rod,

May be found a contrarian beauty
    That appeals to poetical men
Who respond to its call, as to duty,
    Again and again.

Percy Grainger

Some folks are strangely strung,
tuned to the low note's snap and quiver,
fond of songs with a sharper flavor,
licks that burn the tongue.

They love the echoing
of conga drums and booming basses,
shivering skins that hardwood kisses,
rhythm in full swing.

Each beat's a heartfelt thing.
The cymbal as it sways and hisses,
wailing sax and bellowing brasses,
summon up some pang

experienced when young,
some chord too often struck, forever
played in the bloodstream, over and over,
wordless but well sung.

Lawrence of Arabia

I know a guilty tribe condemned to roam
forever in the Wilderness of Zin,
not Jews, not Bedouin,
not free to leave and never quite at home.

No savior makes them pay for what they've done.
They live to starve, and only eat what's bitter;
they love to drink hard water
and labor in the brutal desert sun.

Their crime's forgotten now. That hardly matters
to sinners of their stripe, who pay and pay
and still can't walk away,
preferring to remain eternal debtors.

C. S. Lewis

God, for our own good, is sometimes cruel,
letting blood from the sacrificial lamb,
whether on the front lines at the Somme
or an English school.

His love is fearsome, irresistible:
a love that draws us to its cleansing flame
against our will, until our souls succumb
to its urgent pull.

He is the master, we the little boy
who, kicking and screaming, learns at last to find,
in lessons he has yet to understand,
surprising joy.

Lye

In Massachusetts, air itself
is made of lye;
its wire brushes scrub the front
but spare the lee.

It scours the granite stones that line
the island beach,
corrodes the shells of horseshoe crabs,
blisters the birch.

Displaced, I miss the shabbiness
of cedar shingles
bleeding out, from red to gray
at shoreward angles,

rust that roughens up the steel
of warehouse walls,
the shipyard's reddened gray, the scab
that never heals.

Brockton Man

    In newsprint gray, a friendly face
greets me from the Local section:
bearded, young, with just a trace
of resignation

    tugging at one brow, the eyes
meeting mine – but no, not quite,
they're fixed on something just beyond,
at earring height.

    He's cut his hair, I see. Looks good.
And from a glimpse of neck I know
the rest: the veiny arms he had
ten years ago

    still white-hot, rivered with blue,
the tender skin, still prone to burn.
A headline calls the youth I knew
Brockton Man,

    as if he were some ancient skull,
perhaps not human, scientists
dug up. But modern man can kill
with his bare fists,

    and knives are only sharpened stones.
Excuses, too, are nature's law.
He stabbed her more than twenty times;
her children saw;

    but that was the drugs, my heart contends,
and if I feel a twinge of lust
remembering those tapered bands
of muscle, just

>or unjust doesn't enter in,
nor grief for someone I don't miss
and never having known, can't mourn.
Only this,

>of all instincts, best and worst:
to bond, to bend, to waive, to waver,
to put unruly feelings first,
and gloss it over.

Lovesick

Don't look away, you gave me this disease.
A carrier, you passed it unawares.
My every cell is altered now; each bears
your stamp, a mutant, every drop of me
adulterated. If I could, I'd squeeze
the stinging poison out. It's in my hair,
my fingernails, each microscopic pair
of spiral strands, corrupting by degrees.

Geneticists who study me on slides
could piece you back together. My remains
will carry traces, in these scalded veins,
of your warm hand; in my triglycerides,
and in the deepest etchings of my brain,
they'll find the you my body memorized.

DORE KIESSELBACH

The Painted Hall, Lascaux

Mineral sweat beads patches of the ceiling
of *the Sistine Chapel of paleolithic cave art* –
calcium carbonate
crystallized hexagonally
into cauliflower bumpiness
flint tools couldn't smooth.
In what depends on art
absence must be chosen
not imposed,
so the painter put
the pigment in his mouth –
manganese, toxic in high
doses, for black
and brown, iron oxide
for red ocher – mixed it,
bitterer than March grass
cropped through snow,
with saliva,
sent it to the stone
in tonguey bursts,
the roughness he covered
with his own wet self
chemically identical
to the bones of what his color
led him through.

First Hike After Your Mother's Death

We cross a God-broad field
toward trees, wildflowers
phosphorescing like plankton
in the wake of a great ship,
sign the ranger's check-in
manifest with a pencil
on a string, exchange
breadth for canopy
sunshafts walk through
on long legs when branches
take the wind. Prints
we make in thawing earth
begin to close behind us
before we're out of sight.
The path goes stony, wet
and single file; I watch
you mill your arms to keep
the year's first gnats away,
turn to follow thin squirrels
dashing through new green.
When we pause for juice
and olives amid the fierce
territoriality of butterflies,
you tell me motion unifies
a wind and is its memory,
then move far enough
ahead that you could turn
and see me in the sudden
light as who she wanted
you to settle for, courteous,
with prospects, her choice
not yours. This is where
you disappear into your
new life, but stop and wait
where snowmelt lifts
a sound into the leaves.

ELIZABETH KLISE von ZERNECK

Slant Rhyme

Both sovereign and citizens
of this mysterious and approximate

land firmly believe in the
rhymed enterprise of dark and card.

Here, locate and collate
walk the dreamy streets arm in arm

like cousins, and every
chapel and tavern serves up, in chalice

and stein, its own blend
of aspirin and inspiring. In this slant

and oblique nation, foreign
ears glean symmetry in the clanging

bells of armor and drama.
The local moon looms off and near.

What a sprung, imperfect
place, this kingdom of approximate

connections, where eyes
always know light, where the years

are forever yours, where
both lies and belief can pass for a life.

Illinois Landscape

A quiet fate for the Illiniwek,
their vanished language made of letters long
extinct: strange whistle sounds, dark feathered flecks,
odd symbols passed from hand to hand like paw-

paws, beads, black walnuts. Such bright silence glows
around this language in which the last word
was spoken several centuries ago.
Written against this peeling elm bark, burned

into that buckskin hide, in inks the tint
of plums, orange squash, and sumac leaves, the words
feel foreign and familiar both -- some flint,
some feather-tipped, some arrowhead. How hard

it is to learn to read into their clay,
seed pods, and scratches all our modern sounds.
It's difficult to hear what one can't say,
impossible to speak with no sure nouns

or verbs, although they populate our wild
strawberry patches, ribbon through our stands
of butternut, our scattered flags of thyme
and wintergreen. Illiniwek: thin strands

of language stencil still the trees behind
the flat tract houses out in Kickapoo,
still shape the shaded hospital and mines
of Cairo, form the clouds above the low-

slung strip malls of Peoria. A slow
and quiet afterlife: to haunt the glens
and hilltops, highways, lands once theirs, but now
and newly-occupied with words written

in black. Still, from above, the serifed trees –
fresh sassafras – spell out great green-limbed terms.
The grasses hum a million vowels. The bees
drone consonants. The lakes speak rounds of words.

Science and Industry

I misremembered, thought the walk-through heart
was more sophisticated, more complex.
My shoulders almost brush the sides as we
pass through the labeled labyrinth of veins,
aortae, arteries, and ventricles.
The signage claims this low-tech heart would fit
a human being thirty stories tall.
The children, underwhelmed, prefer instead
the fairy castle dollhouse with its lush
and umpteen rooms, each furnished in detail.
The pantry here is filled with tiny pots,
the dining room with bear skin rugs, the oak-
walled library with shelves of books so small
it took a single paintbrush hair to write
the words. The kitchen hearth is tiled in Delft,
its fireplace aflame with what looks just
like fire. An hour later, in the bright-
lit cafeteria, we slowly chew
our sandwiches while staring at the earth –
a hanging mobile – cut in wedges like
an orange, identified crust, mantle, core.
Some day, they too may misremember this:
believe that hearth held real fire, confuse
the crust and mantle of that plaster earth,
remember arteries as going to
the heart, not from. The earth, a hearth, our hearts:
their multi-chambered halls can often seem
so cramped, their cells so pinched and small. Of all
the rooms we saw today, remember this:
the only one we walked through was the heart.

ANTHONY LACAVARO

An Essay on the Body

Today, in an essay titled *Self-Acknowledgement*
In The Shower, tiny, countless, joyful, Oedipal
Tragedies lingered around the drain, hung themselves
In the corners within which you want to believe
You are alone. *Who doesn't?* Only then
Does the genealogy that brought you here
Come to light: dark contours of the body, turned
From taboos to touchstones, had their own tales
Acting out shanghais like those in the dark ports
Of Malaysia, Old London. You saw the world
In places you least expected, fantastic tales
Of the grotesque and cities moving into industrialization
And away from the fields. Though in your defense,
You embraced your fields and felt a bit sad
At the decision to head in that particular direction.

Babies

When they arrived, any difference
Among them, as simple as
We were, escaped us.
Clambering over each other
Across the land they spun into
A soft chromatic fleshy collective.
They were like little stones
Fresh out of the stream, ears
Folded over like figs as if
To hear only sweetness from the fields,
Teeth tiny as feed corn. More rolled
Forward, collapsing some
Minor civilizations, leaving their names
To be found in the annals of Extinction.
Someone suggested herding them
Into the valley and we did
Until the valley gave way,
Our houses rent from the land and
Only a few landmarks remained
To tell anyone that once we lived here.
And they were crying.
They were always crying.

MATTHEW LADD

Envoi

Our open windows usher in the cold.
    The market falls, and gentle tycoons
postpone their vacations. A billion children flock
    to well-protected dunes

where one can watch the ridleys lay their eggs,
    then leave before they swim away.
Each night is a boat, unmoored, that spins and drifts
    into a waiting day

that disillusions no one. No stray wind
    erases the eye of your cigarette,
and Saturdays once mad with Chardonnay
    are pacified and quiet.

The history books have ripened into fables.
    Only a few old men, their hair-
less heads drawn down in collars of soft wool,
    play hearts in a leaf-strewn square.

Imitation

When I read Philip Larkin
and picture him mugging to Kingsley about WATCHING SCHOOL-
                                                                                                GIRLS
or Jamaican WOGS hawking used clothes in Brixton,
I know this is the year zero

all over again, not because
people haven't changed, or English poets,
but because Larkin is such an unrepentant asshole
and for all that, still beautiful,

like an aging circus performer.
Why are the old so difficult to forgive?
What kind of place have we come to, really,
where doubt racks us like a bad cough

and human feet wash up with the sea-swill,
a few more or less than the day before?
Someone must write it all down, I suppose,
even if no one reads the moldering notebook

whose dowdy author so swiftly convicted himself ...
"And immediately rather than words ..." Ah, Philip,
how impossible the accurate naming of things:
cathedrals, children, the blank self-regard of the bachelor.

Poem for K.

"... a time of thick Bearnaise and mercenary quibbling,"
the tutor concluded, clicking the slide to whiteness.
He always had some salient *mot* for Father,
and he had read enough of Sir James Frazer
to crack a few jokes about pricked foreskin.
"Take my *Homo catullus*, please!" he would say,
or "Heavens! All that vulgar chamois upholstery!"
Like overzealous critics, we lampooned his serge blazers
and ambled about the Arno's marble bollards,
darker than darkness, clever and querulous,
one eye on the weather and the other on each other.
In Copenhagen, at Andersen's cenotaph,
we ate cheese sandwiches and pickled eggs.
In London, the Queen's Guards with their milk-can shakos
stiffened their sabers between our stage-gargoyle faces.

Why did you leave? Was it our view of the Thames
disgorging dead fish like a greenhorn river-god?
That winter, the Brent iced over, its oilskin surface
brittle as mica, tragic, ephemeral.
You settled in Boston, studied, grew sharp as a needle.
How frustrating to realize the distance between us ...
first that failed picnic on the Shuttlecock Terrace,
and now this lukewarm tea, not to mention
my gaffe at last week's chamber concert –
I don't think your husband will ever forgive me.
Your hand, that once rocked my cradle,
rocks so contentedly, these late days, another.
But I wanted only for us to talk like friends again,
K., K., my long-lost, best-loved sister.

Scenes From a Common Life

I. The Prodigal Son

March wind snakes through the pulley frames
    of my antediluvian bedroom windows.
Fear of losing one's roots? Separation anxiety.
    Fear of finding them again – too rare a problem
to merit a popular nomenclature. I settle back in bed.
    A tight-fisted ranch-house slides into my vision,
dragging along the topography
    that spawned all those names: Plainview, Littlefield,
Levelland. Fiefdoms of cotton and oil, "the richest land
    and the finest people." Eighteen hundred miles
northeast of it all, I wrap the blanket more tightly around me.
    My eyes cloud over; my lips harden like clay.

I am twenty-seven years old; the god is not in me;
    all my possessions the dried-up fructure of books,
translucent wool sweaters, matchbooks stowed in mint-tins
    and a photograph of my father at my age, the steam of his tea
twining around the smoke of a cigarette.
    My life pulled from the ashes: realm of the present.

II. Sunday Morning

Sodalities of the Elk Lodge, whose members include
    two alcoholic uncles and an ex-best-friend,
whose mystic rites I visualized, as a child,
    as burning of camphor, as pastry-brushing
of thick elk-steaks, its lot now no more
    than an obstacle to be overstepped
on my way to a memorial, a Requiem Mass
    at St. Ignatius' Parish. Locusts chirr and leap
before me to the door. I sing and pray.
    And lacking the *joie de vivre* of the arthropod caste

lope home darkly. Read. *'What do you make of that?'* asked Holmes.
 'The name of the maker, no doubt; or his monogram, rather.'
I pluck a blue nosegay from my buttonhole.
 Christmas candles with fat waxed wicks
squat on the coffee table in gothic remonstrance.

> *'To tell the truth'* – he sank his face into his thin, white hands –
> *'I have felt helpless ... I seem to be in the grasp of some resistless,*
> *inexorable evil ...'* Isn't it always the innocent
who die too soon, shredded to confetti in the crossfire,
 capped in the throat by a comrade-in-arms with a price?
On the brink of manhood, I have wasted my days in poetry,
 my nights in the cultivation of questionable attachments.

Let the evening go, let it go. There will be others
 in which you are presented with a cassis and soda
in a cut-glass tumbler precisely to your liking
 and asked to develop your views on carbon emissions.
How exhausting to talk to people, regardless of the context!
 The minor flaws exposed, palms perspiring, deflection the
  rule of the day ...
What instruments are within my reach
 I take, and use them. That is the best defense I can offer.

III. High Comedy

Coney Island boardwalk. A steel gate guards the street. Ladd
   approaches
 gingerly. Bolted to the threshold, a missal stand
on which an antique book, smelling of linseed, lies open. He pauses,
 hesitates – *what language* – touches a page ...
SNAP! Bright teeth bury themselves in his wrist; up jumps a blood-
  bracelet.
 And through the salt-startled curtain of his eyes, the words

swim upward to satisfy, even now, his curiosity ... *Italian!* Another
   unreadable language! If only that year in Milan
he had proved more diligent ... A man
   in black hood and goatskin sandals
approaches, pauses, walks onward. Hours pass. Bleating Ladd
   recites a poem from his youth.
Cold comfort. The steel teeth stir, burrow more deeply.

   The shadows lengthen. He has drawn a small crowd.
No more cowled death's-heads, but a clump of onlookers
   as might step out 'for air' on Brighton Beach, c. 1910,
waifish kids in sailor's suits, corseted women with pouter-pigeons,
   beanpoles in knickers and flannel jackets – *God.* He feels
                                   like Christ
trapped in a Graham Greene story: half-drunk, unshaven,
   the pinnacle of health despite his best intentions.
(We must forgive him if, in the future, he sinks,
   leans back to light an apple clove, or rubs the scarred wrist
absently, as one might touch an old lover's
   comb-shell hairclip, hardly recalling its former purpose ...)

Twilight. The spring slackens, the teeth retreat.
   No one to see. He follows the salted grain of the boardwalk
                                   home.

IV. Low Comedy

Situational comedy, they call it, when the best friend bursts in
   on his couch-bound housemates, stammers, "Ph-Phoebe
told me you guys were at Zabar's!" The dough-chested putz
   always making his move a second too early, too late
for the bespectacled girl at the coffee bar to notice ...
   Situational comedy: their jaunt through midtown Manhattan
a foretaste of paradise, where no one pays taxes or loses an arm

in a glass factory, or grows a few minutes older in a bathroom
reeking with iodine. He touches the black cotton to his wrist,
   like an apprentice to the Franciscan friars
in the ateliers of Assisi, mid-Trecento, famed for their mastery
   of colored glass! Yes, if he might capture
those luminous saints in the light of tripartite windows
   cut and leadlined, painted with the appropriate pigments,
vermilion for the Pietá's bright orgy of wounds,
   ultramarine for the Virgin, her straw-gold hair sticklighted
to achieve just the right texture and translucence, yes, *that*
   would be work to aspire to! Though there's no telling, for certain,
that this is how the great windows were made. Supreme irony:
   the monks never wrote it down. Situational comedy:
– *Where's Fra Filippo?*
   – *Dead, this morning.*
– *O Dio mio! He was to teach me the staining of glass!*

V. Intermezzo (Parable of Job)

Job napped behind a haywain, weak from debate.
   In the blink of his old god's eye, his fields
shed their quilts of heather, and turned from purple
   to burnt butterscotch. Every dead stalk
bent low to the ground with its own private burden;
   centuries passed; the lentil plots clicked through their seasons
like cuttlefish. Lucifer sharpened his knife on a stone.
   June broke in a scattershot of warblers. Job awoke.
And having lost everything in a past life, he drank from a stream
   and took up at last the mantle of the shramana.
In the pebbles pressed under his feet, in the bells of Brahmans,
   in the black power lines clattering like yellow-jackets,
he felt the unknowable, the unwriteable, what is left unrecorded
   for lesser minds to contemplate.

VI. The Romantic Sublime

These apricot-pink putti poised with cock-quill pens
    might as well be made of marzipan,
they are so cloying. Only children can stomach them.
    I much prefer the eleven-fingered clothier
jerked from obscurity by the needlework of his poems
    whose threads were woven so cleverly from his blindness ...
Ah! For a life that stretches beyond the pale of vision –
    calendars built on arpeggios! Palm-readings!
The tropism of weekend rambles down the conservatory! There,
    in Jean-Jacques' *petit chateau*, are my beloved familiars
beginning with the thumb of pepper aquavit
    put out this morning on the cracked deal-table –
just enough to rob my tongue of its moisture.
    The gardeners in their denim blouses
treat me graciously, chanting, "We know what it's like
    to have the world at your feet, the pang of responsibility
that comes with years of hard work. Your enemies were wrong."
    In my herb garden, the lavender and fennel
soften the pathways and lighten the French sorrel.

VII. The Critic

    Once more, with feeling. Fate's limestone hand
briefly tightens on yours, then crumbles. Years ago,
    you thought it would crush the talent from you like oil,
your hand cold-pressed to death, proof-pressed to immortality.
    It is not so, not in your lifetime. The prestidigitations
of form you abandoned to 'language-play,' then retreated
    to the metrics of youth, those lyrical afternoons
squandered pumping out sonnets in the green room.
    Now, "L. sweetens his cynicism
with a charming, if puzzled, naiveté." No argument here,

    though he's a far cry, say, from Merrill's *Changing Light*,
whose powwows at the Ouija with Ephraim
    knit so seamlessly ratiocination, clairvoyance, faith in art
and our childlike desire for unfettered communion,
    the fumbling transparent, silly, and thereby lovely.

I stir up my coffee grounds with a pen, and get only
    the thirty-seventh and thirty-eighth views of Mount Fuji.

And I do not love all men and women equally,
    and I do not love all people equally.
Neither can I relax this week, as dust flecks the desktop
    like quicklime, and my father's cigarettes
beseech me from my shallow coat-pocket.
    The coat is not modern; I am not modern;
you see I am concerned with modernity.
    And also with truth, like everyone. The honeycomb
that thrives in the rotten belly of the lion,
    and the beetle's leg tap-tapping along my vitrine
like a crude wooden crutch kiss-kissing the stones of a street
    that winds through a seaside village in a bad Victorian novel.

Marcel Proust's Last Summer Holiday

Balbec's only historical marker
is a 16th-century iron starboard anchor
half-buried in a hectare of Pinot Grigio.

No one goes there. The fishmongers congregate
in martini bars inland from the old city
to drink pastis and sleep with each others' daughters.

In April, a toxic luminescent algae
masses like crown fire atop the breakers;
fish wash up and are shoveled into wheelbarrows.

And when you visit, three months out of the year,
you rarely need to ask questions. Everything
is answered for you already, the gate unlatched,

the shutters pushed open. You confess
things are not always as you remember:
the stalls still prop their skate-wings in beds of ice,

but L'Auberge des Oiseaux, over the off-season,
has renamed itself *Le Harlequin Hotel*.
Marcel, forgive them. You, too, will end up a liar.

Klintholm Havn

Denmark

I have watched the teenagers
late at night, crowding
on the rotted wharves
and in the oystershell
alcoves of the jetties,
smoking vanilla cigarettes,
exhausting their lighters.
When I pass by,
they blink at me
like mute swans.

Tonight, a man is silencing
the lamps along the harbor
one by one, with
a long steel pole.
He walks along the lip
of the sea-wall
like an anachronism.
Behind him, the waves
bare their backs
and melt into foam.

There is no question
of time in this place.
There are only black coffee and oranges,
fried herring
which neither you nor I
can bring ourselves to eat,
and the diminishing
of hopes that, once,
I nursed for us
in this life or another.

Coelacanth

Is it such a crime to stop writing?
We all could burn our manuscripts
and not once dwell on their absence.
The world would be free of poets.
Then I would be at liberty
to sit all day at the kitchen table
carving toys for my children.

How quickly the afternoon fades
when one is well-fed, and has no
elaborate metaphors at his disposal!
Eight o'clock: I turn to the news.
Two Indonesian fishermen
have captured a coelacanth
in the mouth of the Celebes Sea.

NICK LANTZ

The Year We Blew Up the Whale – Florence, Oregon

In that same year, after Lefty Watson missed
his third straight place kick against Salem High,
we rushed the field. Lefty's father, in a black
and orange track suit, shimmied up the goal posts
and, beating the air with his fists, incited
what the *Umpqua Register* would later call
a riot. But the Salem team walked off the field
unharmed, if a bit confused, as we stayed behind
to rip out every inch of turf. In that same year,
when the single-vessel fleet of the Devil Ray
Fishing Company returned with an empty hold,
the owner took a five-pound sledge to the keel
and let the ship sink. In that same year, when
Pamela Reese learned she would never have
children, she stopped throwing anything away,
and slowly her house filled up with garbage,
distended bags of it clotting the hallways, bags
sagging the attic beams, bags overflowing
through the windows onto the reeking lawn.
In that same year, when Ambrose Hecklin's only
son was run over by a pickup truck, Ambrose drove
all the way to Lincoln City, walked up to the first
car salesman he could find, and shot him
in the face. In that same year, when Nell Barrett,
last speaker of the Siuslaw language, died alone
in her two-room bungalow, her estranged son
showed up at the county clinic the next morning
with a mouth full of blood, and though outsiders
would later claim he'd accidentally bitten off
his own tongue in a drunken fit, we knew
the truth before the doctor found the filet knife
in his coat pocket. So when the dead whale
washed up on our beach, of course we tried
to blow it up. The newscasters, who'd come
from as far as Portland when they heard our plan,

were shocked when the blast only carved out
a u-shaped hole in the animal's stomach.
The out-of-towners, who had come to gawk
and jeer, ran for cover as basketball-sized chunks
of whale rained on the parking lot a hundred yards
away. But we were not in the least bit shaken.
If we have learned anything from this, said
our city engineers, standing on the beach in their
gory parkas, it is that we need more dynamite.

Gogol's Haircut

Gogol's haircut is a vast bureaucracy – clerks with fingers
    raw as frozen beets scurry
                      across the Neva of his hairline
into the offices of Nikolai Vasilievich's cramped brain.

    Dear reader, don't confuse
                      the soul with a man wearing
ratty epaulets and a fur hat, waving the handle of a saber
    that has lost its blade. The soul
                      is a mouse, a ball of dust.

In place of a heart a bald hunchback. In place of a nose
    the highest peak of the Carpathians.
                              Hussars for blood.
Noblemen for lymph. For the mustache, a con-artist.

    We can only guess the names
                      of the stories Gogol threw
into the fire before his death. The Man with the Longest
    Name in Russia; The Day
                          St. Petersburg Sneezed.

How can I explain my own *poshlost*, the way I cherish
    the mole on my cheek like a diamond?
                              There's no love
sweeter than the love I pretend not to feel for myself.

    Two policemen patrol
            along the eyebrows. One says,
"Have you seen the Northern Lights, Volodya Pyotrovich?
    I have heard they are beautiful
                          this time of year."

Challenger

The bones of Hannibal's elephants can still be found
    in the Alps. The tilting, prairie
              homesteads where our
tragedies are born will become historical monuments.

    Crows carry off
        the breadcrumbs, and the lost children
have only a trail of guttering stars to guide them home.
    In Vinland the Vikings left behind
              coins, combs, nails.

Max Q is the value at which aerodynamic stress peaks,
    the moment when a rising vessel's
              integrity is tested.
Nothing is a tragedy these days until it is on television.

    The first animals sent into outer
              space died of fear.
A poisoned arrow killed Ponce de León. One day
    a person will walk out
               of his home and not return.

The Millerites waited for God on their rooftops
    like birds wait for dawn.
              The crowds are already
gathering to see the crooked plume of smoke.

    In the deep sea dark, some fish lost
              the power of sight;
some grew eyes big as hubcaps; others began to glow.
    The wreckage of *Challenger* washed
              ashore for ten years.

JULIE LARIOS

Woman with the Beak of an Octopus

She has become almost human, having been a creature
of the sea, multi-armed, dependent on saltwater,
and on certain tidal patterns and marine behavior.

Though she has become almost human, her skeleton is new,
inflexible and strange to her. What she still doesn't know
about air she is trying hard to learn, with neurons

numbering in the billions now, gills gone, her new brain
localized and voluminous. For years, her arms had been
conscious entities, self-directed. That was before the bones

began to grow and the outer mantle to thin, before
the siphon closed. By choice, she left the shallow floor
of the ocean and began to move closer in to shore,

pulled by a changeable sky and the marvel of human sound.
The idea of seasons charmed her, as did the sun and moon,
and her desire for non-attachment trumped the art of suction.

All that is left is to form a human mouth from her beak.
Soon now, she will forget the ink sac, forget how to breathe
underwater, how to forage below the surface, how not to speak.

In form, she will be human, though whenever she passes
a large window, believing it to be liquid, her heart will race
and her hands will be drawn, inexplicably, toward the glass.

Husband, Wife

He resembles a small star, composed
of rapidly spinning light,
and strong east-west winds.
The pressure inside him has a faint ring,
flattened and cloud-like, which
is actually debris from the interior
caused by slow compression.
He swims in the form of a swan.

She is larger, more than twice the mass
of everything else put together. A giant.
A storm system that has raged for years.
She radiates more energy into space
than she receives from the sun.
The fact that she is big enough to hold
two earths makes it difficult to distinguish
between her atmosphere and her surface.

Husband, wife: no one knows
how such structures can survive.

DENNIS LONEY

Flight from the Garden

I could have drowned
but then again you could have said the same
    thing of yourself. What did you see
but cottonmouths through all the sediment?
I thought we had this licked but apparently
the rats still scurry at the periphery.
    Don't move! I've yet to name
internal organs. There, beside the vent,
    panleukopenia. The sound

    of warring clouds
have ceased and fallen into line. The shame
    I felt about my naked body
has passed although these tan, elastic garments
are a bit snug. Because of you I see
a world complete with possibility,
    and since I deferred the blame
to you, I'm sorry. There, there. Please don't lament
    this childbirth thing, it only sounds

    much worse. The grounds
tremble again. Keep moving. See how the tame
    creatures have grown cross-eyed? The seas
are feral too. I'll miss the (time?) we spent
together trimming the garden, but the disease
that trickles from your lip (and mine) warns peace
    won't be easy. We came
here promised bliss but instead received a tent
    to pitch on craggy scabland ground.

Tell me, while all the world's ascream, how you found me
after you crawled ashore: as friend or enemy?

The Man Under the Dump

1. *Aptest Eve*

The night before I died I met the truth,
or rather, the truth met me. It pressed its palms
through furrowed earth, delayed a beat and brushed
away the exponential sense from things:

a cyclone of stars exhaled in unison
and settled on the gleam of a safety pin.
I had so much. *So long* I said to the pots
and pans. *So long* I said to the shivaree.

2. *Invisible Priest*

The seasons change, summer to fall, et cetera.
The wind blows leaves from right to left, et cetera,
and carries the scent from the widow's musky coiffure.
A solitary grackle anchors a branch

above my grave. It sings a rusted gate.
The widow stays. The grackle stays. By dusk
the wind breaks free a few choice strands of hair,
by morning several more. The autumn rains

to sleet to snow, by morning several more.
The grackle stays, the widow stays and both
sing of rusted gates, through spring's first shoots
and summer's brick, the wind unravels leaves

from tangled hair. The grackle falls upon
my grave. The folded silver overwhelms
her thinning hair. The face loosens, the hands
a set of tight angles, all tumble to ash.

The leaves still blow from right to left, et cetera.
The feathers dance along the countryside.
The wind blows ashes, now and at the hour.

3. *Stanza My Stone*

Stones crumble. Papers burn. It matters not
on what my name is writ. The smallest waves
cast shadows too. I walked among the rot,
just as you walk. I studied the splitting graves.

DORA MALECH

Let Me Explain

Spring, and the tulips urged me
stick to schedule, flower furiously.
I asked for mountains but settled
for some flood-buckled linoleum.
Air was the only sure thing
and even she put up a fight.
I called my eyes near-sighted,
my hands near misses, my arms
close calls, my face old hat,
my head a bluff and raised
my body, a wishing machine.
Stars, thanked. Days, numbered.
I wore a coat because you can't trust
weather and I looked like rain.

Makeup

My mother does not trust
women without it.
What are they not hiding?
Renders the dead living

and the living more alive.
Everything I say sets
the clouds off blubbering
like they knew the pretty dead.

True, no mascara, no evidence.
Blue sky, blank face. Blank face,
a faithful liar, false bottom.
Sorrow, a rabbit harbored in the head.

The skin, a silly one-act, concurs.
At the carnival, each child's cheek becomes
a rainbow. God, grant me a brighter myself.
Each breath, a game called Live Forever.

I am small. Don't ask me to reconcile
one shadow with another. I admit –
paint the dead pink, it does not make
them sunrise. Paint the living blue,

it does not make them sky, or sea,
a berry, clapboard house, or dead.
God, leave us our costumes,
don't blow in our noses,

strip us to the underside of skin.
Even the earth claims color
once a year, dressed in red leaves
as the trees play Grieving.

Delivery Rhyme

for Alyssa

As anyone
is apt to, you began as someone

else's symptom. As in
other beginnings: drawn lots, blood,
some dancing on the heads of pins

and inside needles' eyes,
cellular revelry,

hopping
of microscopic

turnstiles. Lucky guest,
grist, leapt

long odds to spark
the tinder in the dark.

Then, the subcommittees met:
made merry in duplicate, triplicate

and so on, much of themselves, divided
and divined and concurred.
All sides insides, pre-ambulatory
perambulation meant: sure

ambit, short orbit
in a warm aquarium set

to the muffled music of a single sphere.
As in other beginnings: parting seas, the future's
violent egress, screams and sutures,

aftermath's average agony
on umbilical belay

but soon to solo, unfold all
those origami limbs to test
the inevitable debutante bawl.

Wrest from the nest
and the rest is you, dear:
dressed for the bright lights
in bits of my sister.

Here Name Your

My friend spends all summer
mending fence for the elk to blunder

back down and the cows to drag
the wires and the snow to sit and sag

on, so all the twist and hammer and tauten
and prop amounts at last to nought, knot, tangle.

The next year he picks
up his pliers and fixes

the odds all over again. There are no
grownups, and I think that all of us children know

and play some variation on this theme, the game of all join
hands so that someone can run them open.

Then war whoops, shrieks, and laughter
and re-gather together

as if any arms might ever really hold.
I'm trying to finger the source – pleasure of or need

for – these enactments of resistance, if Resistance
is indeed their name. I'm trying to walk the parallels to terminus –

call them lickety-split over rickety bridge,
tightrope, railroad tie, or plank as you see fit –

trying to admit to seeing double,
innumerable,

to finding myself beset by myself
on all sides, my heart forced by itself,

for itself, to learn not only mine
but all the lines –

crow's flight, crow's-feet, enemy, party, picket,
throwaway, high tide, and horizon – to wait

in the shadows of scrim each night
and whisper the scene. Always, some part

of the heart must root for the pliers, some
part for the snow's steep slope.

Push, Pull

Coughed and called what bled the quick.
One kick, one trick, one act, one hit.

Called the troops less precious few.
To lift a fist and strike a deal.

To best the jester, cheek to lodestone.
Not rising was occasion of its own.

Spring brought a stiff rain of prostheses,
the storm's black eye on our procession

draped in lace, hook, line, and I do.
Meant charred limbs, rest in pieces.

Meant long time came and none too quiet.
Then, too quiet beneath the birthing

of new galaxies, the nebula's
dark arms of dust. Sun smoldered on.

Baby's first words were friendly fire.
Chrysanthemums of copper wire.

Cat buried out back in a satin hatbox
beside my big broken, obsolete token

I'd taken to wearing on a string. Tried
to trade, but the wind wouldn't bargain, took

more than her fair share of starlings,
left me kneeling on the tarmac,

mouth full of ammo and ipecac,
strange heart in my throat, a belly of swelling.

Bells on bridles to ready for battle.
Broke those horses and there weren't any

horses left. Explosives in the hope chest.
Hawks waiting to be whistled off the fist.

Doused the dovecotes with gasoline.
Slipped the last dowels from the cask.

Couldn't we call the crash a birdbath?
Couldn't we call the coffins gift wrap?

Must have been some misunderstanding.
Shore ordered ocean but sent it back.

Drought Year

Even the sky has its hobbies, cirrus, etcetera.
Cannot rain every day and these days any day

can not rain. The sage and I play
sought and found. I am an amateur

and try to keep my blue above the skyline.
Talk of monitoring elsewhere's mountain,

sighs out of ash, and the meteors' signatures.
Mama puts all her eggs in one chimney again.

A plan for a plan. So breaks our oldest news.
Silence, though "not the void and not contentment,"

where wind writes the grass into yellow italics
and the sky dabbles in sunsets, violent festoonery,

faiblesse. It is the minister of the interior.
I can draw lovely flowers and terrible hands.

Dreaming in New Zealand

I love this tongue as mine (is mine)
and would all were as I am wont
to hear here: sex, a quest, great grail,
for I hear *seeks*, with no sweat spent
to search that isn't *sweet*, as every
beck and call's both song and beak
with which to hold our tune. Winter
wears her well-earned warrior's clothes,
a season wearing thinner, wetter,
colder, but still and ever green, here –
she'd not leave her leaves, not shed
what's hers though the southerly
tried and tries to whistle them away.
And since this is my comedy
of ears, in one and in the other's
fate's to trip again, I'll claim:
the body is both bread and breed,
as words well said are planted seed
and grow so where we tread is treed,
where each line read remains the reed
on which the note is played when pressed
to lips, mouth, self-ordained as priest,
weds *wed* to *we'd* and *weed* and so
with word grown one forever as even
the dead remain in deed, wound round
and round in these wet sheets of wind.

A Shortcut

A hedgehog shuffles out to take a moment
of the moon. The moon leaves off trying on
cloud after cloud to render for a moment
the frowsy foliage and the nose beneath
in tenebrous strokes, not light and dark,
but light in dark or light in spite of.
Doesn't rinse the brush to touch the lilies'
brief white swash and sticky spots
of seeds and pulp where the karakas bend
and drop their drupes. Sprays of stone-fruit
come to sweet rot underfoot with a stench
that in a warmer, brighter hour would draw
the flies to feed at each smear adhered, here
to the asphalt switchback and there to the stairs
that teeter through the terraces and past
the walls that prop the city up above the sea,
walls studded with snails after a day of rain.
The young snails resemble pearl barley, pale,
scattered as at some strange matrimony,
the old are dark burls grown somehow from brick.
Egalitarian spectrum renders the memory
of the sun's gaudy palette obsolete
here where each edge is a glint and each
hollow, a shadow. Holds at first glance each
as distant and as dear, though an eye that waits
to warm to, lets its iris open into
finds that though both take a glimmer, the shell
knows one way to shine and the body, another.
The former's luster, a crystal ball in which
one sees the muddy future, the latter,
a small brown tongue pronouncing "like" against
a concrete palate, careful. Only the wind hurries
here, and the leaves turn aside to let it pass,
shake disapproval. A spider rests
after mending its nets, sits at the center
of tenuous nebula wound from catkin
to fern frond to the black beaks of the last flax,

an almost-still-life. Here a twitch and there
a shiver and each snail's nacreous wake
belies if not progress then process,
illuminated glyphs, transient text, a glisten
spelling if not here-to-there then
somewhere-to-somewhere
by way of these walls that hold the hills from
their someday certain spill into the harbor
a moment more and then another moment
more for each of our small sakes.

CHRISTOPHER TODD MATTHEWS

The Red Balloon (1956)

Wise the way speechless things are,
kind the way faceless things look,
it bobbled down and settled into being,
in the schoolhouse dark, my sweet
impractical companion. Then
it rose and wheeled, nodded
yes from the jumble of rooftops,
traced their slated peaks with its
curious string – and the bullies
in their pulled-up socks shot
their slingshots at it, crowing
and clomping for its weightless blood.

Except, of course, I never was
a Parisian schoolboy, never dwelled
that perfectly in twilight, never
could have paid the kind of crew
it takes to shine the lens with a cuff
or mend a thin-skinned prop. All
I ever really did was throw,
in the schoolhouse dark, my flimsy
American self on the blade of a sadness,
a not unhandsome sadness,
that had nothing to do with me.

My Impacted Tooth, Never Descended

Cockeyed in his palate, as rotten as a knife
in a mummy's gut, clawed to a halt

like a tin-can rocket in this fractious air
of flesh – sure, failure can sweeten

a dull old plan, and there's not *no*
glory in such stoppage – distinction,

some odd power when I menace – but I'm sick
of no food but promise – nearly, as I age,

diseased with promise. Nothing to do
but sit tight and stew, throb in the dark,

not like a seed but a life budding backwards,
born full-grown, a root for a head,

usurped by a baby the shape of a tombstone.
Bright-eyed brat. Sucking at the wound

that I should have made. And loudly on purpose
to bury my scratching.

The Roman Baths in June

Some divine old summer equilibrium
sends English schoolboys to France
and their French equivalents to the Roman Baths in England,
close-cropped blonds in teal windbreakers

surging and swerving like a flock of gods
through the dark of the sunken museum,
marauding like nymphs scattering their light
among the ingenious plumbing. And when they speak to you,

my love, they throw their whole pubescent sparkle
into one English word: *hello*. You don't notice,
do not become more thrilling to my eyes
because of it. But I do, become more thrilling,

briefly, when I respond, as if for you,
ratchet up some crusty thirty-something
oomph, load up some buzz of meaning
into the little word I say to them: *Careful.*

Do you notice these duties I take on?
Do you feel yourself corralled into the center
of this hot little paradise?

NICOLE MELANSON

The Hunted

They are coming,
over the hill there,
eyes bright as lanterns.

What use to ask
if they've seen us?
If they haven't, they will.

We've no better chance of hiding
than the moon,
now caught
in some mountain's embrace.

All our lives
we beg to be held –
why should the moon
be any different?

Still, we run.
This is what our veins have taught us,
the sap in the trees.

We shall run
until we are water

and then, when they are close –
so close we could be their fingerprints –
we shall sink into the earth.

Just watch us give ourselves up.

Becoming Mortal

No bright cry
from the capsized cradle.

No gloved hand
robbing the womb
of its watery child.

A globe of glass,
the ocean smashes.

Now the little mermaid dances,
though knives stitch fire
to her skin.

The history of veins begins
with a fall
towards a marble floor,
and blood as real as flames.

DEREK MONG

Equivalents

Concerning equivalents:
                     lost amid
the Roman catacombs, a priest will halve
his candle flame
                     until one glow doubles
and redoubles on the tongues of terra-
cotta pots –
                     a lesson the split earthworm

learns, as he stands twice the chance of being
split again:
                     a wise move to reproduce
for two worms slither twice as far as one,
which explains
                     why warheads unlock themselves
above a cityscape, thus brokering

a wider
                     higher bloom –
                                   their sanguine hues

and party stars spread throughout the ether.
Are fewer survivors
                     what this division
equals? How does such backwards algebra
apply to the holy
                     whose wafers, cracked
in eighths, constitute a body, though whole

ones add up to crackers? Furthermore, how
am I standing here,
                     by-product of bi-
furcating cells, each one teased in two till
too many pulls

                    spelled *embryo*, and one
    final tug divided *me* from *other*?

Re: Vitruvian Man

Dear symmetric bloke, Mr. Hub and Spoke, what is desire
But a lack between physiques: as in yours, classic specimen
Of men, and mine, i.e. a body? Must extremities measure

Regular as pillars, fit in patterns, or can we consider
My scars, my stutter sexy? I am a creature of incompletion,
Made asymmetric, broke, my limbs speak of what desire

They haven't tasted: my flesh wallows, yours knows flavors.
Do you think Leonardo drew you as an emblem, the one
Man whose body proves (*in extremis*) that man's the measure

Of all things, or should we conclude that all things, whether
Man, muscle-width, or lust can be measured? Did he hear Reason,
That symmetric bloke, Mr. Humble croak: *this is desire* –

"No Man's torso (i.e. 6 palms) will exceed his shoulders?"
Are you a harpsicord, a star, or the most rhetorical of questions?
No man's mind, eyes, or bodies' extremities will measure

Up to your standards. Like most people I will hover
Between plague and pollination, thus tumbling from, unstrung,
Your dear geometric block, Mr. Hub and Spoke, my desires
Mended, mindful. I will sing of bodies, extremities, and measures.

Ohio –

an etymology

comes to us from *oh hello*
Which some believe to mean "I am in a state
Of abbreviated greeting," i.e.: she blinks, I wave,
She winks before the Erie snow

Can melt upon my glasses. Other Ohio
Examples: gravel strafed by headlights, a shield
Of green seen from a cockpit. Explanation two
Contends Ohio grew into a double ode

From a sole, initial blooper: *uh oh –
Oh oh, oh ooooh* my home can speed into a love
Cry or a lyric! Is such ecstasy dubious
when its first note foreshadows

Its finale? Like adolescents and army time, zeroes
Frame all of Ohio's encounters. In fact, some think
We split off from a whisper which went creasing
Through the prairie: *I ow a – O hi o –*

Sisters till a glacier cleaved them? Oh
No, not so. Ohio's as indivisible as amber waves
From rusted pickups. For instance, I have traced
My state's origin back to this abiding sorrow:

It's night, I'm driving with my windows
Down, the cold's encircling my collar. I swear
The earth below me begins to swell and drop
Like three syllables stretched into four low

Then lower letters. The sky goes blank with snow.
I drove and drove into the pages of Ohio.

Mia

niece b. 2-18-2005

Little unclothed
    émigré, did you know
        that after this first day
  a sleep will sink

the bridge
    your body makes
        between your former
  shores and our

unanswered questions?
    So lie still, maybe catch my eye –
    I would like
  to read your pupils,

delicate as candle wicks,
    before they fill your irises
        with color. Will their wells
  tell me if you've begun

yet to remember?
    Do you think I'll see in them
        our shared family, either
  the hundreds

we've both surged,
    like beach surf, from –
        or these tears, the love
  you traded up for?

Somewhere in the shadows
    there, you also know
        what thought is like
  before thought tells you

DEREK MONG

its thinking. Please, for years
    I've breathed this air
        but have never reached
    an answer. Do you hear

birds lifting from, returning
    to a fountain, perhaps
        a faucet dripping? My head
    has shed that sound,

its meaning. Once when I was
    left alone inside a hotel room,
I tried to recreate it –
    one mirror, my best

blank stare, the refrain
    of my name coming from –
        I swore this was so –
    the reflection. The night

was still, the room cool
    as a tuning fork,
but still I knew
    that I was

thinking. Sometimes
    I apply the opposite
        logic, wrap my head
    inside thought's riverbed

and turn on the water –
    Still, such abundance leads
        no more to origins
    than your recent

shore: its absence.
    Mia, It will be years
before I meet you.

Fellini's Satyricon

Released March 11, 1970

Fast forward to Trimalchio, the sausage platter shot, then scroll
through the special features. Can we slow-mo the banquet scene
just when the meat explodes and its greasy bits speckle the stage
    players,
nubians, and albino maitre d'? *Nota Bene*: a certain exotic Other-
ness marks Fellini's cast of extras. Consult the shooting script for
    insight
into this mixed company, what the Romans called *farrago*
and we translate as hodge-podge or cattle fodder and go
about our merry way. In Nero's day the entertainment came scroll-
bound, snapped into hexameters, and set for court poets to recite.
Enter Titus Petronius, the *elegantiae arbiter* and author seen
by Nero's ministers as a nemesis, culture snob, or seedy bard
    whose other
talents remained satiric, from the Latin *satura*, perhaps a play
on *satyr*, though Braund, et al. contend this etymology plays
too heavy on the Greek. Turn then to Juvenal, who coins *farrago*
(see I.86, trans. above) to describe his little books of verse, though
    other
Latin scribes provide variant etymologies. In Diomedes' remaining
    scrolls
he defines *satura* (think saturate) as "a sausage eaten during
    religious scenarios,
the insides stuffed with various ingredients," a line cited
from Varro, ergo *quid est satura*? Rewind now. Fellini's on site
in Rome, canvassing the carnivals for a hundred human oddities to
    play
Roman demigods and generals. *Nota Bene*: In the Ceres Temple
    scene
a *lecta* (trans. carriage) wobbles on the burly arms of six *spago*[1]
as they herald the "Hero of the battle of Quadragesimo," a role
given to a quadruple amputee (see *satura*). Don't bother
to trace this shot, excess from the fragment of a tale that's other-
wise non-narrative.[2] Better to blame Petronius whose unsightly
suicide (wrists slit, sewn up, then slit, see Tacitus) left the scrolls

of the *Satyricon* to the worms. The undigested parts became a play-
ground of forms: prose novel, picaresque odyssey, a *farrago*
of verse. Scholars stitch it up, trim the fray, but like Hollywood
    scenery
the fake clouds still look fake. So with what we've seen
what have we learned? *Conclusion 1*: fractured texts are other-
worldly, the classics "a nebulous galaxy"3 where brave men go
to die. *Questions for future analysis*: How do I cite
the booklet for my DVD? Should your average screenplay
include all, a lá the sausage chain, or is The Satyricon just bloated
    scrawl?

---

[1] The *spago* (trans. eunuch) scene was never scripted, but shot (a total fluke) on-site.

[2] Would you work to adapt the work of another? Do I own a film when I press PLAY?

[3] Constanzo Constantini's *Conversations with Fellini*. Go to *Film, Italy*, or *Satire's Role*.

Period

Cicero, In L. Catilinam Oratio Prima: 254-58

July 2005: as regards
                        two Humvees crisped

like matchboxes on CNN, leading a congressman
to claim, and with the same voice
                                  he taped six months ago,
that the meaning of this loss will become evident

if we hold out one more year –
                                I too wish none of it

were true, for what are we to do when the language
of the state begins to ape (it flirts
                              toward all it lacks)
the language of seduction? *We won't leave until this*

darn job is done, sounds less like a duty than a death
sentence –
                Period! And though they wrote
the war's cause off, the hawks still garner faithful legions.

Autumn 63 BC:
            M. Tulli, quid agis? –

Cicero, Roman consul this year, begins to speak
in *impersonatio*, his voice
                            hangs from a leash
within his grasp, feigns the Republic's tone, then turns

a question on its master. Neither his answer
nor the query now matter,
                            save that Catiline's response
must be guessed at in the margins, and the State's sentence

 (it translates subject,

DEREK MONG | 203

                        blood and verb) knots its clauses

noose-like, delays its winnowed meaning: read period.
What writer wouldn't be seduced, become
                                                    complicit?
Dallas, just last summer: I'm standing beside a man

(God, he must be
                        nineteen) who wears our state upon

his sleeve and feels its boots walk him wherever it says
he's needed. Our airplanes
                        wait, his lover sobs, TVs
hum like word balloons above us; in them five men speak

of foreign threats,
                      their bodies framed by pillar after

pillar. Hours pass, the soldier sighs, I read a book
to keep from looking.
                      I wish that none of this
were true, that the heartland grew question marks and stopped

taking the bullets
                    it's been given. As it now stands

my mother's last best Ohio friend answers every
Apache crash (her son
                      pilots them) with valium,
dissent expends its last nuanced breath, and word after

word is hollowed out
                    (*patriot, terrorist*), strung into

the same delaying thread, the great deferment
of climax.
        Yesterday, I came upon a painting –
it was Judith, her arms awash in blood, cradling
the head, the half-bit

tongue, of Holofernes. The maid

is there, the knife glints silver, scarlet. Here is the part
that's missing:
            her tease, his hushed oh please,
the slow verbal seduction, which despite her looks, his lust,

remains the sharper
                    weapon. Holofernes must have known

that this was wrong, that somehow this was what she wanted.
Still, he walked to the slaughter –
                            M. Tulli, quid agis?
In Rome they're roiling in the death throes

of their Republic.
                Within the month Catiline's five

conspirators are dead, choked by the State outside
the Forum. Their leader lives
                        another few weeks (maybe
hears Cicero elected *pater patriae*) before

he's carved up
    with his legion. Do we know

now where this sentence goes? Can we translate *auctorem
sceleris*? Somewhere a typewriter
                            stalls; some guns
are jammed but smoking. I have not placed

one useful word between them.

SIERRA NELSON

We'll Always Have Carthage

Your head must bow to your heart,
which is why I always look down;
if the earth is round and round
I'll be wrong until the ends of it.

Beautiful, you said, and meant
the sea. Reminding me –
there are walls to be built,
rocks carried.

Now I can't meet you
or your eyes – just the boats
below in the harbor,
burning.

The wind shakes the earth
from its four corners;
the flames are picking up,
or is that me shaking?

Look, I'm right – the sun is underwater.
Now get out of here with that lion's skin
on your back.

Orvieto

Giddy on major life decisions
averted – free! – we take
the funicular up the mountain.
Is this the Italian hill-town
famous for its boars?

"On my left shoulder, you will see
a beautiful cloud," a tour-guide says.
Rice in the cobblestones,
we stand before the gothic sunlight
and squint up into molten gilding.

We are paying for last night's
good dancing in bad shoes.
In shady corners,
teenagers make-out with jaded abandon
and we suppress thoughts of afternoons
and earlobes, speak casually of
the wine of the region, admire
the tufa.

I long for a home where I could
use this giant platter
painted with lemons –
present to you a fish
wrapped like a bouquet.

Maybe you could learn to play
the accordion from that boy
who only knows one song
but plays it very well.

The city gets sleepy and closes
all its shutters,
except for the underground tour
of medieval pigeon coops.
We'll take it!
Our guide directs,
"If you look just under your head,
you should see a little
passage of steps."

The sun is flirtatiously
slouching toward the horizon.

Be sure not to miss
the last train back
to the life you thought you wanted.

MICHAEL LEE PHILLIPS

Teaching the Romantics

How old do you have to be before you can elope?
True question.
Girl had her hand up, front row, peaches and cream cheeks,
something less between the ears.
Imagine Shelley's heart getting passed around. Trelawney
hamming it up, strutting. Military bravado
always gets them. Byron sulking
somewhere in the back row, leching on the girl to his left.
Keats? He was yesterday, and this is all
pretty much a drag. They've seen these guys
before – that pyre on the beach,
the mighty hands that ripped a real heart
from a squishy chest cavity – all part of the tour, dude,
like this was before
they were even born: yawn, yawn.

Oh, but that girl – she wants to know about elopement.
Let's take a serious look
at some of those who tied their knot early.
Let's start with the old greats: Keats, 25, Shelley, 29, Byron, 36.
And you know what's coming: James Dean, 24, Kurt Cobain, 27,
Marilyn, 36,
John Lennon, 40, Brian Jones, 27, Buddy Holly, 22,
Sylvia, 30,
Richie Valens, 17, Big Bopper, 28, Sam Cooke, 33, Hank
Williams, 29, Otis Redding, 26,
Elvis, 42,
Tupac Shakur, 25, Heath Ledger, 28, Robert Johnson, 27,
Bird, 34.

Okay, okay. I hear you – you want to know what this litany
of the dead is all about – what's your frickin' point,
as you so eloquently ask.
The point is that these people took some heavy vows
before their time – you understand that, you logoed-up knuckleheads?
Think about this: Jimi, Janis, and Jim, 27, 27, 27.
Now, there's a lottery number!
These people eloped for good with a mate they can't divorce
and now they've got a question for you.
And believe me the chorus singing this question has got some pipes!
This is the question that Hamlet wanted to skip,
the one question everyone will answer.
Take your time on this one people – soon as everyone
gets quiet. Thank you.
Remember, one side of the paper only.
Okay, here it is: *How old do you have to be before you can die?*

The Man in the Barrel

The man going over Niagara Falls in the barrel
changed his mind half way down
and nothing was ever the same again in the theater
showing the news reel of his barrel – hardly more than a black
smudge in the grainy black and white photograph
the stopped film became. It was hell getting the man out of the barrel.

People remarked for years that a mind should never be changed
in the midst of such an eventful undertaking.
And this was impressed upon the next generation of children,
whose minds were never changed, not once,
after they decided something.

The man who changed his mind in the barrel
never changed it again. Once removed from the barrel, he lived
an obscure life, unable to convince anyone
that changing his mind was more important than completing the ride
over the falls. After all, he argued,
many had ridden barrels and even other contraptions over the falls,
but no one had effectively changed his mind
in the middle of the fall.

You have no idea, he would argue to those who remembered him,
what it took to change the mind
after the barrel had ceased buoyancy and plummeted.
You try it, he would say. Try stopping
everything that shifts you into the next moment – especially if
you chose that moment – try pitting your own
lump of gray matter against all the known physical forces propelling
you pell-mell toward the one thing you most desired
above everything else in the world.

And look at the people still sitting in their seats staring
at the barrel that won't fall.
They've been waiting all this time – what should we say about them?
Should they be told the truth?
Should the man inside the barrel get up on the stage and tell them
that the mind inside the man in the barrel
has been changed, and that the barrel they see before them
is never going to fall, not now or ever,
and that the one thing all their minds expect to see next
is something they will never see?

Shooting at Lamar

Bob and I have .22 rifles and as soon as we fire
a volley that goes zinging over the hood of his truck,
Lamar stops and we can tell that it spooks him.
It's summer. Maybe we're seventeen, just two guys
cruising the desert hoping to while away the boredom.

We fire some more and the rounds spit up sand
all round Lamar's truck and some go whizzing barely
over the cab – the whole time I'm wondering why
we're doing this, all of it seeming kind of stupid.

But we keep firing and then Lamar sees who it is
and gets out his own .22 rifle and real quick
we have those same bees buzzing our heads
and the sand is going splat splat around us too.

Christ, but this goes on for a long time, and all
the time it feels just as stupid as when we started.
But the fun of it has taken over and there's no way
in hell we're going to stop, not having this much fun.

And we keep having fun and we keep shooting
and the bees get closer and the splats get closer
and I remember thinking – one more foot, then another
foot – how close is this going to get? Starting to
worry that maybe it's Lamar who decides that now.

JESSICA PIAZZA

Kopophobia
Fear of fatigue

The pension in Prague had no alarm –
we missed the early train we stayed awake
to catch. My fault, our doomed attempt to sleep
in shifts; I thought wouldn't doze mine off.
For us, no clear, Hungarian lake to see
the sun's eclipse; it shadowed us outside
the train, out-dulled by clouds. We caught our breath
in Budapest and fell in love – adored
this city, thriving on its brokenness.
A new museum, but burned-through tenements
were testament to how destruction does
not mean the thing destroyed was beautiful
before. Those dragging weeks we built and razed
each day, and nothing that we made endured.
Our statuary garden songs were frail
as monuments composed of candle wax.
Your sketchbook left on the Bazilka floor
like trash; my notebook sloughing ink in rain.
It was a mess, but we make art that's made
for drowning. On the bridge by the Danube,
that storm deluged the city as we ran,
outpacing it until it caught us, sang
staccato rain into our hair and fled
too frantically ahead. I never said
I loved that broken way you looked when things
went wrong. I should have. And I can't forget
the fire-chewed bricks, the statues saved from riots;
how they braved ruin, but we could not survive it.

Melophobia
Fear of music

They'll tell you there are only two ways: flawed
windpipes that knock like water mains behind
thin walls or else a lovely sound like wood
winds sanded smooth – no in-betweens. They'll find
you practicing your scales, determined not
to fail. A voice too frail, too thin, begin
again, again, again, now overwrought,
now undersung. Not done. They recommend:
just sound as much like *you* as possible.
But we know *possible* is slippery.
Your Oklahoma: like an ocean filled
with earth. My Texas: ocean filled with sky.
Sing into a conch: you'll sound like yourself.
Sing into a conch: you'll sound like the sea.

AARON POOCHIGIAN

The Marriage of Peleus and Thetis

Death is an evil – so the gods have judged:
had it been good, they too would die.
– Sappho

Petty as we are but more beautiful,
the goddesses could only squabble
over a gaudy bauble
and call us dull.

But we the drab mothers, the wedding-planners,
stood aloof and shrugged at their bad manners.
The world flipped upside-down: though bound to Hades,
we snobbed Heaven's Empress and the fancy ladies.
Gods were like mortals, mortals like the gods –
we paid them back in condescending nods.

They won all, though, and all we lost
by dying rankles
our ghostly bosoms: tossed
tresses, clacking bangles, dancing ankles.

Kudzu

    Strictly Japanese
at customs, he reached out, held
    our gazebos, trees,

    porches and houses
helpless in his jade embrace.
    With all those spouses

    sporting his strange name,
he wound up naturalized
    and at length became

    an up-and-comer
on hills, in hollers, greater
    summer by summer

    until Dixieland
felt small. Whether he picked up
    this itch to expand

    from shoguns back home
or rooting through our heady
    American loam,

    the will to wester
tingled his tendrils and now,
    a vast investor,

    he claims by a clutch
Kansas, Oregon even.
    He is just too much.

    He is too far grown.
We must complain about him
    as one of our own.

ALISON POWELL

Shangri-La

Draw me a hangman's portrait. Draw me a fine girl
in the river. Draw me against the black of your eyes.
Draw me and what I give – lips drawn, still singing.
Draw Shangri-la, you did, did you, the year you left
with only the blues, lucky, but still. The fine girl
in the grass. We've been laid down, yes-yes, say yes,
a mouth rubbed all in tequila and sea salt, a famished
belly and you kissing it. And shadow of limestone,
and the barn, and mazes out of corn stalks. O
tanned – what legs! Inside your jeans.
Draw each thing that keeps you breathing, draw
your kitchen sink, draw a bath for coupling. My,
I still love you, am drawn to your wicked ways,
to your sleepy ways, to your underwater, tiny,
sweet ways. Draw me a mouth, a red red mouth.

Decorum

A person could be at a loss. The width, spools and yardage, meringue
airs, impossible long fingers, of decorum. Its army sashay of the side-

walk. Iguana-eyed, left on stoop, no knock or ring. The small blue
 bruises
on hard heels a person wouldn't get because you wouldn't run triple

down the stairs to answer. Because to lift the unbashful marble, ah
 it's lit
differently, the arm would straighten. Door and doorbell taking on
 a low

religious typewriter drone. Stomach rot of rose milk and rubbing
alcohol. A person makes a habit of not knowing what to make of it,

as fact is, most days no door or invitation wants opening.
The table crowded with its nestled chairs. Eyes close at a glance.

Edema

My father says, *They might have to cut it off her*. Simple, like bone
and bone, her finger has fused with that old ring. She sits there,

mindless as plank wood, cawing in a starched hospice bed.
They'll use a tiny saw to do it, split the band etched near the knuckle.

Her slippered feet swell, too. Unpredictable boat-blocks, they hold
inside one move, nothing *swing*, nothing called *fox*, just one blue
    bee-

line, dreadful and straight. We take her wrist and crowd the bed
and we encircle her – ghost of leanness, muscle blown, skin

no more tissue than wind. This serum is serious and mean.

The Raw Fields

A boy is raised up in the raw fields.
He knows his hard feet in the husks.
He knows his mother, her bottles and naps.

Knows his brother's war dreams, is afraid
to sleep next to him. His father has a way
with the jitterbug and a whipping switch.

There are kindnesses: the giblet-
thick dressing of his grandmother,
the pictures of Venice in his schoolbook –

the gilded water. How the fathers
look in their Sunday best and the prayers,
like milk, around him.

One spring day the great god of his dreams
descends and, exploding, fills
the new tar streets with rainwater.

He exits the high perch of the linen closet
where he has been for weeks reading
and pushes out into the storm.

All around him are the old lives of leaves.
Oak tree sticks make lean-to's
without being asked, school is nowhere in sight.

Though there's water-weight to his knees,
he pokes one thin toe into the gutter. Here
he knows there is desperation, devotion, hard

loss. He opens his arms to the fierce yelping sky
and cries back *Oh! Great harbor, I am
your tin ship!* before his mother, weak

in her yellow slip, yanks him inside.

CHRIS PREDDLE

Water Sonnets

1 A Body of Water

The old Turkish road that we walked to Lithi bay
was so bouldery it would've unhorsed a bey
from his chestnut or bay.

That beach in Greece, both stony and sandy,
was where I longed like a song for you, Danny for Sandy,
as the waves slid up and down like glissandi.

Rupert our guide was asleep in a cool place, Brer Rupert.
Margaret your chaperone left us, whom the dragon ate, Saint Margaret.

Behind my back, alas, you addressed
the business of getting undressed
as the waves came up in a wavy line, their long rank not dressed.

We entered the Greek sea,
a body of water curved to your own body, like a C.
We swam further than anyone could see.

2 Waterwife

You liked to swim when the windsurfers' wind,
the *ora* of Lake Garda
uncombed your hair like surf unwound
from the lake's breakers and combers.

Waterwife, between wind and water, come back. I guard you,
beached myself. The waves are as high
as our coom-
ceiled attic, my ivory attic high and dry.

From my uttermost attic I bend over the sill
like an ingrown nail, and look for you, lakelady, far-off in the swim
of things, a skelf
of your swimming self.
Even the attic with its *sprezzatura*, its airs in the swarm of air
must surf the wind like a boardsail.

3 The Sink

This ruin is the Baths of Cleopatra, so said
our Greekling guide. If Cleo patronised

such a minor
Roman municipal facility on the coast of Asia Minor,

I'm the Emperor Theodore. Its stones sank
as the sea level rose. We never thought to have sunk

so low. Lo, below your swimming form
the ruin looms, said our cicerone, like a Platonic form.

Indeed. Whatever underlies
our Christian civilisation and the lays and lies

of East Rome, however the migrants and Muhammedans
(as the Emperor says) have hemmed us in,

teach me, Jacqueline, to swim, not sink,
above this sunken rectangle which waits like an open sink.

Not Catullus

for Ken Walker

1

This ruined villa never belonged to Catullus,
you'll be disappointed to learn. These five acres of overbearing
    masonry,
of arches, porches and porticos (the scholars tell us),

this belvedere the height of a dozen Romans
were beyond your poet's pocket, their sumptuary insolence
too much even for him. Though they stand on the heights of
    Sirmione,

his darling eye of islands and peninsulas,
a promontory, as he might have put it, poking into the bottom
of Lake Garda like Silenus' penis,

this was not the homestead that he came skippingly home to
from his labours in Bithynia, not where he wrote of the crisis
with Lesbia. The owner of this pile with a lake for a moat

was a cross between Caesar, Pompey or Crassus, and Croesus;
the barge he sat in, like a bum-burnished throne,
burned up the water on his cruises.

2

We've made it home to the world's-end Britons, their world-
 without-end north,
and it's you passing our front gate, six foot six
in flip-flops, bearing down on the mailbox. Yourself, none other,

would fit that generous villa, not merely for an excess
of inches – you who travel continents
from school to school with stories from the Tiber, Euphrates and Oxus,

in Roman dress, a senator in a schoolroom; you who happily consent,
for one who is dying, to be her singer of tales,
reading aloud to her all the novels of Jane Austen.

The Arrowloop

The archer at an embrasure
had an outlook like ours here at the back, narrow
between our bathroom extension that intersects
the sky like a bastion, and next door's massy gable-end
at a salient angle. I see no more
than Tim's hollytrees that march
like a curtainwall over his meadow, the holegns and hollins
that gave their name to this vill of Holne
in *Domesday*. This is as much
as I see when I write, this mere
locality, this little Walden Pond
on which we do as we can, we skater insects.
His small view compels the archer at an arrow-
loop as he warms his hands at a brazier.

Earthmover

Richard in his field drives a hired loader
between a dumptruck and his spoil-
heap, and digs away at the established order

we've known from our window, that bank of earth and ordure.
Its topsoil,
or whatever he's driving at with the tyre loader,

is colonised by grasses, foxgloves, rhodo-
dendrons and a Chinese parasol-
tree happy to dig in, their self-established order

like a peace. He has felled a forest of cedar
sweeter than oil –
he's having a field-day as he drives the tireless loader,

Gilgamesh in a Lada.
I stretched in the medicinal milfoil
and hoped – but he digs away. He has disestablished the order

of us who sat like Buddha
under his banyan with its trunks in a coil and moil.
Richard, in the field of words they derive the tiring loader

from Old English *lād*: a leading, a road or
journey, a carrying. By toil
you hope to dig away the established disorder.

Follow-the-loader, follow-the-leader,
sing not here the pastourelle.
Richard in his field contrives the tired loader,
the heap is dug away, he has re-established order.

Ruin

Smurry smoory smeary rain
is blowing down from Holme Moss and its moor
on hawthorn, rowan

and holly or holme, on sheepwalks, on cattle red and roan,
on us. Jacqui and Chris, Mary
and Ken, we bend against the windbent rain,

which comes at us and our roofs, shutters and rones
in combative waves like an army.
We live (we live well) in the policy and reign

of an emperor (Imp.) of the west, who runs
like a rain gutter around the limits of things, whose humour
affects us (imp!) like a murrain.

He arraigned (aroint thee) and overran
Holme and Babylonia and the Country of the Living. Errant Sumer
he made a ruin.

First Letter to Ed

Awaking one's lute, Ed, goes back to a psalm:
    in the Prayer Book David
with a lute sings praise in adversity. We're less divided;
let us praise Thomas Wyatt and sing harm
    to adversaries and animadverters. When we're devoid
of comfort, wake up, lutes, no longer keep
    your late, loutish sleep.

All things averse to me, all animus and afflictions
    (though with his lute George Herbert
sings that by such our sinful nature's inhibited),
all these harm me only, with melancholy fluxions
    and malignant humours. I inhabit
a malcontented spot, with lute songs on a shelf
    but nothing of myself.

I admire, Ed, those who are whole, of a piece,
    like Herbert's country parson,
sin-carrier, priggish, but altogether his own person
(well, his dear God's). Grant us thy peace.
    We in adversity have personae
in verse: you've been Hakagawa and a Scottish Sufi,
    I am anticke Sappho.

Somewhere there must be a suitable image of Sappho
    with a lute, a fairer Wyatt
in travesty. If we are whatever we make, whatever
we fabricate from the diverse perverse reverses we suffer,
    we know what we're for.
Poetry is making something, Sappho's *poiesis*,
    and we've made a couple of pieces.

All our inverse outcomes, all the animosity
    of the cosmos, were never the converse
of the self. Whenever our dissolute lutes converse,
without Herbert's priestly habit of theodicy,
    and disparage this disappointing universe,
we conserve the self. What counts, Ed, is the fact
    that, better or worse, we act.

Awaking Jacqui, her body like a lute, from sleep,
    or talking with you as far
as we walk in a day, and learning of another as fair,
I'm held in a community, as Little Gidding would keep
    and comfort Nicholas Ferrar.
Each night they'd read between them, as if linking arms,
    the complete cycle of the Psalms.

Cattle Console Him

1

    Cattle of consolation,
come down, cattle goddesses of five hundred kilos,
sundisk bodies, bellies, digesters of cellulose,
    come down to my anxious field.
    Once before you filed
into the frame of our picture window, ate our windbreak
of Cupressocyparis leylandii, spoke, and broke wind.
    Come to me now, tell me the solution,
why it's here or there that a cow occurs
in a random field, why you're moved without cause.

2

    Boethius in his prison
saw no cause for the headfirst destruction he would suffer
or the king's Gothic cruelties, until Philosophy
    herself came below
    and nudged his writing elbow:
'Give up your headwork, reasoning and knowledge, Boethius.
It's divine providence.' Let her not console us both
    with a gift grown upon misprision.
You thought you were one of the Sun's sun-gilded cattle,
but he sold you off to death, less good than chattel.

3

    Thomas in his cell,
a monastic cell in Windesheim, who seems to imitate
not Christ but all experience, counsellor and intimate –
    you know how sharply I'm aggrieved
    by the shortcomings of others, how grieved
that my own happiness comes short. Though I will not seek
dead Christ pinned out like a cattle skin,
    how much, Thomas, your book consoles us.
He endured great trials, says the *Chronicle*. He was buried
in the east cloister, by the side of Peter Hebort.

4

    The cattle console me.
We are no manger moocows who bend the knee
at midnight, but hardier. Like us, be here and now,
    mired in the flesh hocks-
    and-oxters. Turn ox-
wise at the end of every furrow, pull the oxharrow
of your human nature. O her hair is oxlip-yellow,
    her body curved like a meadowgrass, a culm
of grassflowers. Love her, like herself, whatever occurs,
be moved as cattle are moved, love without cause.

Groundsel

I am at the door-sill, the ground-sill, the very groundsel-edge
of old age.

Age-old Greeks,
already in waiting to be shades of Hades, already geeks

of their own language and intellect, were the first to make this
    metaphor.
What they meant it for

was not the initial going in
to the anteroom which is old age, but leaving again.

*

Common groundsel, Senecio vulgaris, with its seedhead
like an old knight whitehaired,

was used in poultices for toothache or an abscess.
There's no old remedy for absence,

or leaving. At this doorway I've no more to do.
Let me go through.

BOBBY C. ROGERS

Burning the Walls

I took the torch to work today, the site
on Circle Street, that tall frame house you dreamed
we'd someday live in. Remember the Sundays we drove
through neighborhoods finding dream homes?
We don't do it anymore. We hardly get up
from the kitchen table and never speak of
the thirty-year note or moving from this shadeless street.
I paint the houses we looked at and could tell you
about their insides. You say I don't make enough
for my effort. Does anyone? But this is work
I understand. I can follow the repetition
of long brush strokes, the governed paths of the roller.
Everything I know is just motions now
and the getting through them, how you say goodbye the same
each morning, leaning to not touch
my painter's whites that hide a million spatters,
how my hand always finds the same place
on your shoulder, the other hand
the same place on the enameled door frame.
The house on Circle Street had to be burned.
Have I ever told you why that is done?
Paint builds up. Twenty years of exterior oil base,
every new coat a little less even
until it has to be burned from the siding, and you start over.
If it's done right it is all new.
You would be amazed. I've taken off paint and found wood
still green. I swear to God sometimes
you can see the pencil marks
left by the carpenter's helper, the black stamp
of the Weyerhaeuser tree. The nail heads
will be gray and shiny. You can count the circles
each place the nail was driven too far
and the hammerhead struck.
You say we never talk and you know nothing
about what I do or how I feel about it.

I will tell you this. I spent all day
on an aluminum ladder. My hands are shaking
from holding the propane torch and keeping the flame
the right distance away. The paint doesn't blaze
at once. It wrinkles like apples on the ground
and slowly a bubble comes up, the first oxygen
getting beneath the paint. Then it burns.

Nocturne

To be heard in this house we must say the words as though
    cutting them
into polished stone, phrasings hewn to resist what the night will do.
    Even at this hour
the table lamp's bulb can scribe only a loose circle on the floor, its
    yellow light
pushing against the corner shadows, the slurred last note of a one-
    note work song.
Everything has a voice. The words we use fly from us like chips
    and fine dust, settling
on the toe moldings and window trim. If we move with enough
    care we can live here
for years and stir nothing at all. The tops of the picture frames
    wear a velveteen husk
of dusty apology – a gloved finger would peel up a story I told you
    one night in August.
The few things I am sure of must be said as quarter notes, an
    iteration so slow
it will become hard to recall the first faltering word where the
    sentence began, back
when you were still listening. This city is never quiet. At midnight,
    every night,
the cargo planes begin their scream and strain, somehow
    shrugging their way clear
of the black earth. It is hard to tell when the sound of one plane is
    gone and another
takes its place. God knows where they will set down again. I
    believe there is no erasing
what is said, even if it goes unheard and unheeded. The words will
    gather
somewhere. It's hard enough to know what we mean to say, and
    that isn't the half
of saying it. To find what is speakable in my heart will take all
    night. The best time is just before
the darkness splinters with new light, the dawning ready to be
    sectioned by the bent blades
of the venetian blinds, opalescent lightstrands to lift the night's

weight from your skin. It helps
if the words are simple and worth saying. It helps if the first thing
I say is your name.

Pastoral

I find that, as I grow older, I am becoming less susceptible to those feelings of deepest melancholy that used to come over me when I looked at nature, and I congratulated myself on this as I walked along. – The Journal of Eugene Delacroix

Most of the time I don't even notice the grainy afternoon light
    cutting across these uplands
sharp as a drawknife peeling back the day's veneer, laying it open
    until there's nothing left
to enclave my recollections of all the other days lit just this way.
    To you, everything is simplicity
and sweetness out here in the country – bean fields and hopeful
    small towns, a two-lane highway
climbing a hill, then gone. I have no idea why I ever came back to
    this latitude. I'll be walking
to the post office, happy with the sound of my shoes hitting the
    sidewalk, reprieved from a desk
in a windowless room, and the light out of a mild sky on the
    thirteenth of May will look exactly
the way it's supposed to look, exactly the way the light has looked
    on every thirteenth of May
I've ever known, caught up in the greeny penumbra of the red
    oaks, laid out across the soybeans
rowed in Mr. Brooks's fields, marking me. This is what home is, a
    few shapes on the retina
that won't unburn, certain sights sifted out, weightless and finely
    cut as the sky's shiny litter
of cumulus piling higher once the afternoon comes on and heats
    up. For the most part,
landscapes are imagined, anyway, chlorophyll and sky tilt,
    honeysuckle and magnolia blossom
loading the wind with a regret savored mostly in the mind. What
    of it is real? The mockingbirds
bicker in the fig tree, and the jays scold and hiss, but they've
    ceased to sing before I'm done
hearing the note. We build our impressions from the scattered
    sticks of lost afternoons,
one minute raised from the wreckage of the last. The sky and the

    landmarks we've learned
look innocent enough, but they're a front for all we thought we'd
    buried by simply outliving it.
There's something painful pooled in the furrows and drainage
    cuts, heaving up the sidewalks
and blacktop. The past is crowding against every bit of news. Take
    the smell of that lawn, mown
this morning to a uniform height, cut too close from the look of it
    – what comes into my head
is four decades done. If I had the time or the inclination to look
    more closely, it's possible
I could find something of beauty, something unremembered and
    immediate. But nature's peace
is a worrisome thing, an itch turning my mind from the task at
    hand, so much information
encoded on the back of the wind, brought forth in the quality of
    the day's duplicitous light.

Newground

We would sometimes take the old road home, the unlined asphalt
    sun-brittled
and load-riven, as though our forgetting were just another of the
    elements
wearing down what's in its way. All summer long the tar had wept
    out in tiny dribs,
blood-black like the ones I imagined on Christ's Gethsemane brow.
    We were in the country,
white pump houses in the side yards of the old homeplaces,
    briars and scrub woods
pitted against the seasonal order of rowcropping. We passed a
    field afire, tongues
of flame the size of tongues edging out toward the road's gnawed
    shoulder.
"Burning off a newground," my father said. I was so young I could
    hardly see
over the dashboard but I knew when he said something just to
    savor the sound of it,
some tired regionalism, a dying word's bended note. What was a
    newground? Something lost,
I supposed, someplace worth lamenting if you had a moment. I
    was coming to suspect
all words had once held a meaning I could only guess at. Most of
    what I knew was just suspicion
which I was hoping would harden to something more
    dependable. My father didn't need to watch
the road much to drive it. We'd rolled the windows down: the
    smell of a place
would linger in the car for a mile or two after we'd put it behind
    us, honeysuckle and cow piles,
the smoke from the field stubble caught up in the heavy air. By
    the next time we passed this way
a disc-harrow would have turned the burned-off field, its ashen
    crust buried
under coppery new clods of earth carved as smooth as the way
    you might remember
a woman's bared shoulder, or the gently curved waves in an old

        vacation photograph, neatly rowed
and back-turned against a whitened sky. The ash will wait for the
    next crop to leach it
from its dark bed and feed it to the sun, purified. Enough time has
    passed. I can tell you now
what a newground is, and I know that clod and cloud were once
    the same word,
but there is a cache of words that were my father's and are not
    mine to lose or love,
the way he would toss them out the open car window into the tire
    whine and wind roar,
that beautiful road song I'm trying to sing for you, the last miles
    between here and home.

JOHN SUROWIECKI

The Hat City after the Men Stopped Wearing Hats

At the inauguration no one wore hats, not even
the poet whose hair the wind shaped into a fin.
We sat at the kitchen table trying to figure out
how we would make a living now that the river
no longer flowed carrot-orange to the Sound.

We used to tell the children that its fish wore
fedoras and suffered from mercury shakes,
twitching, lurching, losing scales as we would hair.
Every street used to be a river of hats and when
a war was won a sea of hats would suddenly appear.

Every day we'd walk to work leaning into the wind,
hands on our hats, and never once did we think
the factory doors would close and never once
did we notice the frost late on the lawns
like an interlude in a slaughtering of moths.

Connecticut Invaded by Chinese Communists [1951]

Through our basement window I saw
the world as a worm might or a cricket
or the dead. I thought there must be
a hole in the earth that began in China

and came out at last into our midnight,
under our stars, where only our Big Boys
and blue cabbages stood between us
and their ruthless, mole-faced men.

I thought their bayonets would smell
of meat gone bad and feel like fire going
through me. My blood would accumulate
in small pools, forming small rivers,

and bullets entering my brain would
empty it of dreams: dreams of children
with holes in their heads all ready to be
hooked up and yanked out of life.

The Childless Couple's Child

Every now and then she dies of leukemia
or is carried away by chocolate waters.
Sometimes she's a blur under pond ice
or in their arms when their jet falls from the sky.

In all this time she's spoken a dozen words,
their words, but in a breaking, desperate voice:
utterances of incalculable loss, the tragedy
brought home, a sense of what it must be like.

She's always lighter than they remember
and frailer and more bashful, never asking
if she'll be given a name or a place in their hearts
or if there's ever been anyone else.

Americanization of a Poem by Wislawa Szymborska

No one in my family ever wrote a poem.
My father's laughter, because it was so rare,
was a kind of poetry, as was my mother's
acceptance of everything ordinary and out of luck.
The broken embrace of a cousin, once a boxer,
was never exempt from pain because of nights
spent in pursuit of a string of words. We speak
in a language that's mostly holes anyway
and so we say in a thousand different ways
that we work without getting rich, that we fall
into old age as an acrobat falls from a trapeze,
that we fight our wars in remote places where
flies are the size of Windsor knots and yet
we only smile when we see each other with our
grandchildren who look like us all over again.

The Wisest Aunt, Telling the Saddest Tales

1

They give her lunch, prick her finger for sugar.
Her stories are usually about being unlucky:
a young soldier is given away by the steam
from his own urine and so on and so forth.

2

During the war it was easy to find piecework;
after the war, it rained the names of the dead.
On her place mat is a map of the world: Canada
is a pink peony pressed into the northern seas.

3

She was the last to hold her daughter's hand;
death entering her had the sting of nettles.
When she was eleven she saw a boy's head
crack like an egg and a gray yolk spill out.

4

A phoebe builds its nest under an awning,
sky-blue and cloud-white stripes like her robe.
Once, against regulations, her son brought
her strawberries: O how delicious they were.

5

In the TV room, *Search for Tomorrow* is on,
the volume too high, the color all wrong.
How can you search for something that's
certain to arrive and just as certain to pass?

MICHAEL SWAN

Not What I Meant

Food and water were plentiful.

I had a little house
made from the boat's timbers.

I got up every day
before dawn
because of the spiders' webs.

Have you seen spiders' webs
with the dew on them
in the early sun?

And in the evening
did you know
the colours on the clouds
are exactly reflected
in the surf?

And the moon, then
makes a line of gold
from the beach to the horizon.

I knew all the birds,
the small animals
and the trees.

And there were porpoises.

The only sadness:
such beauty
and no one to share.

One day, a ship.
I jumped up and down
on the big rock.
I waved my flag –
a shirt on a stick.

'Come and look!'
I shouted.
'The spiders' webs
the shells
the blossom
the birds of paradise
the moon!'

They took me away
and gave me potatoes and beef.

I said 'No.
No, no.'

They gave me new clothes
and cut my hair.

I said
'That was not what I meant.'

I told the TV people
about the porpoises
and the shells and the blossom.

I told the doctors
about the spiders' webs
and the line of the moon.

I said
'Yes, I waved my flag
but that was not what I meant.

That was not what I meant.'

How Everything Is

Perhaps this is how everything is.
The scree steepens into rockface;
you work your way up ten or twelve pitches,
each worse than the one before,
the last a brutal overhang
with few holds, and those not good;
somehow, pushing your limits,
you struggle through to the top
with your arms on fire,
to find a car park, toilets and a café.

Hendrikje Stoffels

Silly, isn't it?
A moment's encounter
in an art gallery.
Our eyes meet
and I think we both realise
it could be important.

It doesn't happen to me very often
(I don't know about you)
and I'd like to go further
(I think you would too
in a way).

It's a pity you're not free.
If things were different
maybe at least
we could manage a weekend
or an afternoon.

Don't keep looking at me like that
through your frame.
Don't you realise, girl?
Don't you realise?

Some People Get That

It was smaller than I expected:
more sort of cosy.
Semi-detached.
Beautifully kept.
Lovely garden,
but ...

'Look,' I said,
'It's very nice, but
I imagined something
I don't know, more ...'

'You have no worries,'
they said.
'There are no doubts here,
no conflicts,
no jealously, failure, sadness,
no losses of loved ones.
No fear of death.'

'Yes,' I said,
'I know, but
wasn't there supposed to be,
you know, joy,
beatific vision,
sort of thing?'

'Ah, yes,' they said.
'Some people get that.'

Lance-Corporal Swan

Boys' Brigade
All London Challenge Cup 1923.
My father on the left:
Lance-Corporal Swan,
18 years old,
pill-box hat, cross-belt,
smart as a sunrise.

The photo over,
they swap punches,
have a smoke,
chat a bit,
head off home.

Out of the gate
he turns right
and walks whistling
down a winding road.
Behind a tree
amputation stands waiting;
round the corner
my mother moves into ambush;
at the second bend,
doctors aim their stethoscopes;
up the hill
madness crouches in the bushes,
swinging his great cudgel.

BRADFORD GRAY TELFORD

At the Theatre

– for Darin Ciccotelli

We went to the Marinsky on an evening in late June.
Our box hung high above the pit, an expectation.
The conductor bowed. The English horn spoke Russian.
Curtain up on Chinese lantern, Chinese moon.

*

I wondered about the cherubs, what had they seen?
Had they tired in the plaster, their paint and gilt wings?
What bores an angel more – violence or beauty?
Why bother when the program changes nightly?

*

I go to the theatre to forget I'm at the theatre.
I go to the book to forget about the shelf.
I go home to remember I'm a stranger.
I go to you. Remember me. Forget myself.

*

We didn't know what we were seeing.
The chorus sang of nature. A shepherd mentioned grace.
Bulbs flickered in the wings – sheet lightening.
Gobo net the stage in gold-green lace.

*

The actors churned these foam-core scrolls.
They looked like deco-fenders. They were supposed to be waves.
Theatre happens in the brain's soft coils.
They behave the way a churning sea behaves.

*

I was nine – a thirty minute Czech operetta.
Children, wolves, a storm, a stalled train.
The children wanted out, the wolves wanted better
than the wind and the snow and the Czech refrain.

*

I go to the theatre the way Frost went to the woods.
Often I don't like it. But I do feel better.
I work for the theatre the way Rilke worked for Rodin
what with his cold and attitude and thin, bad sweater.

*

The shepherd wanted nothing – that's his job.
The kingdom wanted peace. The drunkard out of jail.
The set designer: more gold, more silver foil.
The emperor would catch the nightingale.

*

Art may be a meeting between a man and his work.
Once there he speaks – he plumbs the heart of "is."
A moon will glow. A deer will learn to walk.
There is no self without artifice.

The Woman Who Was Not Matisse

This is the story of the woman who was not Matisse.
I knew her doctor husband, both her daughters – there were no
    sons.
What there was was design, execution, a white Maltese.
And there was a garden: crape myrtle, potted dill. Caladiums.

Caladiums were for Texas for they flourished in the heat.
The dill was for Russia – it drank a lot and needed shade.
A patio in brick, slivered with koi, good teak.
A Baltic ivy trellis in a green-black-black-green braid. *Braid.*

You want a story fine I'll tell you a story.
Her daughters were choices, as was her husband, ditto her black
    clothes.
Ditto each wingback the spine of each book the light the
    rosemary
the floating iron pots on one of two steel stoves.

So everything was perfect and everything was grand.
I'd never seen a thing like it and was half in love.
Her rigor – her edge – her black eye – her white fierce hand.
So many of us alive not knowing how to live!

But in her house there was no color. In her house, no art.
Light woods, dark woods, black-white marble tile.
Silverspined books by Proust and by Sartre.
But no print, no watercolour and no (no, God no) oil.

One day the daughter's harp had been refurbished and delivered.
The inlaid soundbox. The curved blonde shoulder. The ravishing
    neck.
And the woman made them take it away when she discovered
all the pedals re-felted warm pink instead of black-black. *Black.*

Later the daughter told me over drinks what had happened.
One day thirty years ago the woman made a choice, a kind of barter.
She'd put away her paint, drawered her work, banked her stipend.
For life was short and hard. And art was long. And harder.

She'd realized she wasn't Matisse. What more do you want?
She knew it would be better. Real life. With different dreams.
And this will happen to you and will happen to me or maybe it won't.
The house has been in magazines.

from Excerpts from a Dream House

The Conversation

We were drinking Diet Coke and talking about our dream house.
Inside: Birdseye maple, concrete floors, pin-spots, his-and-his and
    his-and-his.
Outside: rot, weeds, jays on a soon-to-be-downed wire:
design within nature within desire and desire.

I drew a box and you drew a box and we had two boxes.
My father always said *build more house than you think you can
    afford.*
You like color and comfort and nothing too weird.
I like hundreds of rooms – big, empty as Texas.

We kept at it with crayons and rulers and colored papers.
I showed you mine: stick figures, smiley faces, lots of big orange
    hair.
You said you were frightened of the pet purple monitor lizards.
You kissed me and we made love for an hour.

Then you drew a bedroom with ivory walls, bark trim, one
    spectacular window.
Ten steel clocks that showed the season and the minute.
Maybe I would quit smoking. Maybe you would win the Lotto.
We closed our eyes and made our bed and slept in it.

Regarding a Backsplash

We gathered up our shards for the mosaic in the kitchen.
I sorted them by shape while you hand-mixed a caramel grout.
I called you "groutiful." And you were. And I was smitten.
You said you'd always grout me. "Nuh-uh, no way – " "No grout."

I picked up a piece. "Oh. God," you said. You said, "it just so …
    gleams."
You said anything more perfect would just be wrong.
You said we were making beauty from the fragments of our dreams.
"Keats," you said, "and Oprah say that's how to get along."

"Maybe," I said, "it is the shape and color of my love for you."
The color? 'Iridescent Rainbow.' The shape: a four pointed five-
    point star.
A broken figure – breaking toward the real, the true.
"No grout it's beautiful. No grout exactly what we are."

You said "The fifth point is invisible because it's the future."
"It's there. We know it. Only we just can't see."
You kicked me the bucket as I velveted the hammer.
"I'll do the future. You, the present – please – carefully."

I tamped those four points gently in the grout.
You built a fifth: blue agates, shales, a thong of hammered tin.
That night my poor star jimmied loose and then fell out.
That night my future came and put it back again.

Portrait of the Artist's Mother at the Analyst

The mountains are lovely. The people are not.
And life's a longish novel short on plot

that folds, unfolds in delicate vignettes
of men and women, beef or fowl. *So*s. *Yet*s.

That's what I know and what I know can kill.
I know the mountains, know their sad vaudeville

of beauty much like most people I've known
whose lives encase them like the icy chrome

you see on all the better mountaintops.
In early evening one drives by bus stops

and almost dies – people – how might they live
without knowing you? *You*? Your need to give

some jonquils or a photo of yourself
to each one of them so each life itself

contracts a mythic sheen while clammy love
evaporates like those thin clouds above

my mountains each spring. I have yet to meet
the person I'll become, whom I shall greet

with that love I've long withheld from others.
I am in hopes that one of us recovers.

from Four Trees

Melia azederach

When we cut back
your mother's chinaberry tree
she didn't quite cooperate,
didn't go peacefully.

Storms were coming in.
A storm was rolling out.
I Googled her.
I like to know about

a thing before I do
it harm. *Pride-of-India,
Texas Umbrella, Persian Lilac,
Bead Tree* and *Japonica* –

a name for every home.
A crime for every alias.
I clicked her yellow fruit –
rock-hard, poisonous –

cut her leaflets – *toothed, blue-green
and toxic* – dragged along her bark –
a *curative though deadly*,
pasted *the buff, hallmark*

fissures wrenched tight
across her purpled torso
elongating her pain,
a late El Greco

(though each spring she'd burst
in *drooping lilac panicles*).
Your mother wasn't well.
Sport utility vehicles,

two of them next door
plus a brand new fence,
the storm, her terrible cough,
impeccable evidence

that the dead limb –
one of three in the trunk's braid –
would cleave off easy
(wrong – again). I was afraid.

Lyric and decorative
foreign-born *Melia,*
a transplanted Ruth,
invasive, diligent Medea

wild as the bow saw bit
into her soft back.
We got her down,
her snapping twigs black

with your blood and my blood,
the sheeted sweat, the flecks of skin,
a ritual we'd do once
and be done with and then

you watched me jump.
I crushed her spine.
We left her by the road.
What's yours is mine

and what is mine may well
be yours. I think. We're both givers.
It was late.
We looked down: ants, carpenters

sifting their wreckage,
dirt, dried pith, broken phloem,
pale larvae clamped tight in black jaws.
There – there was the poem.

September

Warsaw, 1939

I guess I was the quintessential "lad."
They said my having little meant I had

it all, this life before me stretching out,
an endless pocket endlessly turned out.

Then planes, fires. Then the first battalion.
Then night and smoke and then mere oblivion

sans teeth sans eyes sans taste everything I
used to sing I used to sing I used to sing.

from Self-Portrait on a Need-to-Know Basis

For Further Information

I think about my work every minute of the day. – Jeff Koons

We want to be loved for what we've created –
not for whom nor what we are, not for how
important or precious or devastated
we, at our core, might be, although now-
a-days speculation on this core
would have us all made real by perfect hurt –
our dear gaping uncovered in the desert
outside Taos where the sky and mud floor
of our world give unexpected way
in a thousand-foot drop of sheared basalt
broken like a bottomless argument
into layer, fragment, contour, and fault,
into what we did that molten day
our great rift opened and begat this moment.

JAMIE JOEL THOMAS

Towing Water to Australia

You can want whatever you want
and still another tenth of the iceberg
gives itself back to the ocean;
you can say things are perfect, right now,
exactly imperfect as they are –
the trees one rain away from busting
their seams – but then the daylight always
hammering itself into the next
cold-engine morning, clouds gathering
on a horizon that even the quiet
can't keep quiet – and you can't
be blamed for asking things to remain
familiar as the last word and new
as the next one, just like our words
can't be blamed for meaning both
where have the last five years gone?
and *there is one thing I want and we're it.*
You want to walk so slowly
under that canopy of singular leaves –
those days in a single day – so intent
on not disturbing the dust in the sunlight,
that everything filters down
bit by visible bit. You want
to quick cut down anything that comes
between you and the possible horizon.
What you want is a trail of freshwater
stretching nearly back to the South Pole.
So what if they can fashion a life
in an incubator? Give it some time.
Give it a driver's license. Put it in traffic.

Youth Longs to Live

which is a kind of dying, the same way a match
is a kind of darkness. Sometimes words
end up in the stickiest situations, as in the phrase
Your chocolate is in my peanut butter.
Sometimes the agreement is to disagree;
"mass" is used just as often in church and lab.
And just when I think that we aren't ultimately
adding up to what MBA's call "redundant overhead,"
not just one massive, decaying proton,
some 40-something in an orange Stingray
swipes the parking spot that should've been mine.
The supermarket far, far away, half the planet there
to pick up milk or eggs or bread, comparison shopping
for just the right brand of bottled agua.
Call it luck or a lack thereof, but someone out there
thinks water from the Swiss Alps
is decidedly better than its Canadian counterpart,
thinks the best milk is furthest back on the shelf,
a later expiration – "we'll see who cheats who,"
says Orange Stingray to the grocery store.
Only they don't put the milk out
before they have to, opting instead to keep it
on ice, a mass of shivering subatomic dairy particles,
in the cooler, in crates, upon which sits
an oily 18-year-old staring out through the skim
at the expanse of his *stock-boydom*.
He's killing time, wondering how
the gods must've felt after stocking the shelves,
fronting the product, sweeping up the storeroom.
Life, to him, is a case of warm beer
smuggled out the back with the night's trash –
and if he's not eating a ham sandwich,
surely he must at least be thinking of one.

MATTHEW THORBURN

Now is Always a Good Time

Between the Age of Enlightenment and the age
of thirty, I lost my way. Disappointment

scuttled down the breezeway. Ennui stretched out
across several white wicker chairs. "Beauty,
closely apprehended, breeds fear," I told myself

by way of reassurance. "Then sorrow, then loneliness."
Then I felt better. Poor L.A. Where could one turn

without running into a pink-tinted martini,
a kiss on each cheek, that hankering that follows
the hankering for gin? Oh, for an ice cube

and something to plunk it in! I lip-read the director
as his leading lady tucks into the duck pâté,

the duck canapés. "The world's too twilit,"
he seems to say, "too black and white." The yellow
bowl of arugula sits unnoticed off to one side.

Who loves lettuce? But Hoagy Carmichael does
a funny thing at the piano and my heart

swings open like a Murphy bed. Now a hint
of stale Nag Champa tickles my nose, or is this
Chanel No. 5 letting go of someone's taut tan wrist?

I know no one wears it anymore. Things change –
we'll always have that. "I liked it better,"

someone says, "when the world was flat."
That someone is me. "I agree with everything
you've ever said or thought in your life."

Me again, but headed home. *Ma petite amie*,
Jeanne D'Arc, rolling over like a wheel of cheese –

what are you doing still up and smoking in bed?
Tonight, the stars are quoting the collected
works of Howard Hawks, word for word.

It takes us all night and all morning. We watch
and watch. We drink it in like gin.

Horse Poetica

The one I rode in on. That mud-colored nag.
When he blinks his black eye bigger
than my fist, his eyelid's an upside-down
pocket. And the scrape, the spark of horseshoes
on dry rock – each sound has a silence
tied to its tail. Or else it gets penned up
in the mighty barrel staves of his ribs.
Oh, but *staves*? That makes me
hear music. That tinny harmonica, that tuneless
squeezebox, the song we ought to know
better by now, but still follow for days
down a path that's only a path because
we believe it is. Now where'd our giddy up
and go go? My horse can't canter. I hop along.
We've been outfoxed. Farmed out and fenced in.
If we were given a chance, then given
a second chance, we'd both choose a paddle
and a boat and float. Soggy but saddle-less.
We'd both need new names.
Then new shoes. Meanwhile, we hang
a left at the one-armed cactus. There's another life
after this one, but it's just as dusty. Meanwhile
we're caught in a crowd of cows and cowhands.
But they part for us, they part like a Red Sea
of beef. Then they get going. Then I get
the bit between his teeth. Then he bites.
Boy, could we use a minor catastrophe or two.
Let lightning like a lasso streak straight at us.

Gravy Boat

I wonder who wound up with it
in the divorce – and notice immediately
how "wound" looks the same
as *wound*, a hurt – that tacky
ceramic number, tricked out with leaves
and grapes, I picked off the gift registry
at Marshall Field's and actually saw
hard at work once – full of bubbly
steaming brown gravy! – on a Thanksgiving
table, oh, five, six years ago. It's the name
that grabbed me, a boat designed
to keep liquid *in*, that frail coracle
that carries not necessity, but condiment –
this rich, salty blend of meat drippings
and flour in the original, whisked up
right in the pan, or some processed, jarred
whoseywhat from Wegman's, nuked
and on the table in 60 seconds flat.
If I had any say in it, it would've been flung
at the wall – finger-pointing, yelling,
goddamn it, a ducked head
and crash! – in an after-midnight
fight months before anything was "settled,"
the paltry goods divvied up, boxed
and trucked off – what's left
hauled away to what's next. Let it be
one more victim, shards
of green and brown on waxy
linoleum, swept up, binned and gone –
to be dumped and forgotten, left to crumble
into dust and blow away into the dark
indifferent waters off Staten Island
from the landfill called Fresh Kills.

Self-Portrait with Unmentionables

A nubbly pink throw rug breaks up
the butter-colored tiles. Avocado toilet and towels
and here are the tell-tale *Glamour* and *Cosmo*
peeking out from under the Kleenex box
atop the toilet tank. O shimmery shower
curtain (mauve, salmon) jammed to one side –
Bonnard, you'd be happy here. Closer up, the green
neon of the mouthwash. A squiggle of cinnamon
floss pokes out of its plastic case. All
framed in the gold-framed mirror, I see now,
along the top of which steam disappears, so it only
takes another second to figure out I've only
just missed her, and make out the many whites –
pale pearl and eggshell, sea salt, saltine –
the flimsiest of whimsies hung up to dry.

Woken Each Morning by the Glad Laughter of Birds

So long, skydivers. Who jumps
out of a perfectly good plane
even in a dream? Hello blackbirds,
are you blackbirds, ringing in
my wake-up call – *Konk-la-ree? Oke-
ra-lay!* – but too quick on the wing,
like luck, to say for sure. Here
and gone, unlike this afternoon's
watered-down watercolors. They stay
all day. Gosh, how beautifully
boring. Even the greeneries – well,
just *green*. So rain falls. Things grow.
Big whoop. Does yoga stress you out too?
Too much water in your watermelon?
Hang on, Lulu. I love seeing how,
arms full, you close the car
door with your hip. You sexy problem
solver. But I should be helping,
not seeing. I don't want you to be
a symbol or an image. Just be.
With me, please. And now? Let's do
what we do best. The watusi,
the shing-a-ling. But why am I still
talking when I'm wanting
to listen? May my ear be a dark room
on a sunny day, cool enough to draw
you in. May we be blessed only
with what we need, that slippery
something non-chemists call chemistry.

Horn of Plenty

Like this paper horn of flowers tipped
across an arm. I'm jostled, poked
with it – it's how happiness happens
here in the subway. Asters to zinnias
and violets, deep oranges, crenellated
yellow and cream, the faint brushwork
of babies breath, a frill of green
and I'm off now, past the turnstile,
the stairs, and into Astoria. How's this
cornucopia work? One thing plus
another, and repeat. Say a boy in a red
suit with a birdcage on one side,
a cat on the other. Like the boy is
blond, the suit too short – and what's
in the cage, where'd that cat go?
But that's Goya. Try Gershwin. This is
Steinway Street. Let's say everything
green. These ladies' saris, mint green,
sunlit against the black-green, deckled
green hedge. High in the tea-green trees
each green nest awaits a green bird.
Or like the coffee klatch of sparrows
outside my window. Each morning
they file this reminder: *you're human,
you're human*. And everything else
I can't shoehorn in here, piled up like
the fish, pale pink and dark pink,
stacked row upon row in this
fishmonger's ice, beneath the swirly
frothy cherry blossoms. I'd let it go
almost, I would, almost all of it now
to have what's next, right here, what just
makes it into my eye – that flicker, this
watery light, that bit of distant tinsel
the magpie drops everything for.

Still Life

– Pierrre Bonnard

That he would go back
after hours to retouch
the ones hanging in the gallery –
he must have had an in
with the guards – to get it *righter*
if never right, you've heard
before. How he'd revisit
the light – bring it up
or turn it down – just as I have
returned to this morning
all afternoon. They make me
hungry, these two pears
he must have hurried to paint
so she could eat. A few green ideas
about grapes. The apple
shows off its high bald head.
To be fascinated by fruit.
Not fruit, but light. Imperfect mirrors,
imitation mirrors. His broken
pinks and reds, green and
yellow mottle, this dash of white –
no, *light* – no, canvas
showing through. I almost catch
my face there, looking back.
I know this fruit. I've eaten it
all my life, though this basket's
new to me – a few brown twists
of vine, uncertain transport,
but I'm moved. I'll say that.
Made to speak. Such
tenderness, his abiding
affection for anything touched
by light. And he needed

so little. A few pieces of fruit.
A window. The sky
trying on every possible blue.

D. H. TRACY

The Explorer at Eureka Dunes

Found them. Sand enough to levee the Amazon.
Make buckshot of pearls. Then rustle awhile
in forever's hourglass. So fragile
they calve under the rat-treads dusted on

before daybreak. But sterner than the rock they used to be.
Able to handle the climate better.
Geologically hell-for-leather
the great aisles shiver downwind. In their lee

dunegrass and primrose, unaccountable. Some will want
accounting anyway. Pressings. A sketch
of each. Conjectures of what the milkvetch
does in other seasons. The transit and the sextant,

my plain-dealing emissaries, will not fix them.
I'll lay them back in their cases, neat,
having put the height at seven hundred feet.
That figure – wrong already, growing wronger, fiction –

will not credit much the received portrait. My report's failure
does leave the local strangeness intact;
I will have folded away its fact
into my spare and private republic. Therein a danger

maybe worse. Imagination wants them free,
higher, brighter, would have them prove
that reverie will not remove
them from themselves. I have no general dunes in me,

only those seen on the visit. If a child
should want to hear a desert tale,
the being-there might not avail
the teller. The being-there might not avail the told.

AWOL

Our slitted eyes accost him, where and when
we have nothing better to do than make
a sacrament of our own industry.
At bus stops and in line. Our chiding eyes
have become his element to weather,
a condition. Other times, we only watch,
from shop windows, the concrete sanding down
his sneaker soles, or glimpse him
wading the medians and culvert-grass,
thumb not out. The young deserve discomfort,

which is why we put him in the navy.
We have changed, though, his linens at the hostel,
washed the ashes off and patched the burn-holes,
and fingered the ragged edges of the envelopes
kept in his pillowcase. We picked off the floor
his matinee stub bookmark. We also have been
the too-skeptical bunkmate, and tales
of jumping ship have rung, not false, abstract.
Abstract. Magazines lie in his lap,
absorbing him. The wayward deserve

correction, but ostracism will not work
in his case. We have tried to bring him in,
giving him free refills, and throwing him
a flirtatious word to liven his campouts
in the corner booth, and remind him
what he has given up. His gaze extends
out the filmed windows, down to the harbor;
he eyes the great gray eminences,
the aircraft sulking on the decks, the white-
liveried hands, deserving, he might think,

to be torpedoed to fuck-all. We have made him
look the miscreant without trying to do so,
though we have tried to do so. He has paid
with nickels and dimes for cigarettes, and lingered
at the station counter turning out his pockets.
We have begrudged him twenty, fifteen,
ten more cents, and pressed into his hand
the several small victories of ease
he will win among us. The streetlights
lay down their capes for him. The willful

deserve comeuppance, or envy of their will
would rule us. Then there might be no place to take
leave of. He has set his elbows on the railing
of the bridge. He has very slowly chalked his cue.
He has pulled a cap around his ears and left,
but is never absent. He has scorned
our elected futures, that seem to him
hobbled for the choosing. We have set
the outlawry. We have muted awe
of his taste for panic. He has not said uncle.

BARBARA LOUISE UNGAR

Embryology

Could it just be hormones,
this euphoria
as if someone rubbed petals

of opium poppy all over
me, inside and out,
or could it be true

what the rabbis say:
when sperm meets egg
two angels enter to teach

the soul that floats,
growing, in darkness –
one angel holds a candle

so the new being can see
to the end of the universe
and back

and when lessons are through,
one angel taps
three times the upper lip

and departs
as the babe, in travail,
fights its way into *The vale*

of Soul-making alone,
and marked,
having forgotten everything.

Riddle

There's a penis deep inside me,
    getting bigger every day.

I'm growing balls
    & big teats at once.

I'm of two minds, two mouths,
    four thumbs.

I've got a pair
    of hearts.

Twenty toes &
    twenty perfect toenails.

Hair up & down,
    & lanugo to boot.

One womb, one way
    in & out – the hard strait

he'll have to take.

Matryoshka

You move in me as I
in earth's strange atmosphere,

as her blue-green ball spins in the expanding darkness –

within me, you cannot fathom me,
as I can't see the globe I tread, but feel her

warmth, her motions rocking me

to sleep, her rest in which I wake, and she
never dreams in whose body she sleeps, turning –

like Matryoshka dolls, the next nesting

in the last, we grow and do not know
how or who is holding us, yet we are held.

CODY WALKER

Update

My latent superpowers, well, they're back:
obliterate a marriage with my mind;
bewitch the president, that lying sack
of – Cody! Take it slow. In time I'll find

– please note, I'm speaking as my therapist –
the equilibrium that time affords.
I've also rerouted (I have a list)
(1) my neural pathways and (2) some fjords.

America's a country for the lonely,
the loony. Whitman said it years ago.
Remember, he could fly and he was only
an editor, a wingèd bearded schmo.

My powers have increased a hundredfold
since you left. Maybe a thousand-, all told.

The Cheney Correspondence (Selected)

Dear Dick Cheney,

Today I could barely leave the house. I flipped through magazines; I ate crackers; I checked my email (a lot). Do you sometimes feel that things are both important and unimportant? Now I'm at a coffee shop, but the day's basically over. Imagine being forty, but still feeling like a character in a sketch. Hope all's well with you.

Yours truly,
Cody Walker

Dear Dick Cheney,

When I was younger I wanted to be a baseball player. But I can't remember whether I loved baseball, or whether I just wanted everyone to love me. A confession, then: I still want everyone to love me – blindly, entirely, without sense or reason. Even you, whom I've regularly excoriated.

Fondly,
Cody Walker

Dear Dick Cheney,

I'm going a bit bald. Other than what it portends – dotage, death – it doesn't bother me. I'm also getting fat, which does bother me. Have I told you how beautiful I find most women, especially from a distance? I keep circling back to this line from Whitman: "What real happiness have you had one single hour through your whole life?" I hope you won't be too offended if I say that I have difficulty picturing you making love to Lynne, or to anyone, but I can easily picture you in a bathroom at three in the morning. I don't know how people picture me. Maybe with a pen, and a clutch of flowers, and bile in my throat.

Warm regards to you and your family,
Cody Walker

All Poetry Is Political

Arnold Schwarzenegger
stepped on a beggar
woman, then gave her a signed photo
of himself and Gary Soto.

Carolyn Forché
sat in a bookstore café,
practicing her thirty-yard stare.
Because: spies, everywhere.

Walt Whitman
didn't hire a hit man
nor blubber the words "heckuva job"
when – Hey, what's that thingamabob?

Dude, that's my heart!
And the funny part
is that it's half dead with fear
and half Edward Lear.

Earlier Today, Archival Edition

Thinking the microphones were off, Secretary Rumsfeld
Yelled
"Kill kill kill kill kill kill kill" –
Jokingly, we think, but still.

Offenders

Karl sat at the table, carping.

It was always *something:* Richard's amnesia-thwacked groupies; Richard's opium pipes ("Illegal!" Karl would remind); Richard forgetting to mention Friedrich had called.

Richard rolled his eyes. If Karl, that nut-job, wanted a piece of him – well, he'd be right here waiting.

So it went with the Marx brothers.

"The Mould of a Dog Corpse"

a l'Antiquarium di Boscoreale, Pompeii

It's not a promising title.
And his legs straight in the air: they give pause.
But I will swear this dog is laughing.
Mouth open, ears back,
doubled over
like a drunk watching late-night television,
he is hysterical,
he is funnier than a volcano.

And
he's a visionary:
he sees me, immortal at thirty,
and cannot, cannot stop laughing.

Bozo Sapphics

Bozo, Toe to Toe

Tilt the glass: the terrorist turns to freedom
Fighter. Likewise, clowns, in the funhouse mirror,
Stand as kings. Self-interested theories on which
Bozo calls bullshit.

Bozo's Imbroglio

Showmen, offered tenderness, tend to take it.
Husbands know this. Tickle a clown: does he not
Laugh? Then why subpoena him, why inflict more
Pricks on this Bozo?

Bozo, Woe

Bozo's six apologies, five excuses,
Four rebuffs, and three switcheroos are met by
Two deaf ears. Behaviorists gather, call this
First-order clowning.

Rebozos

Scarves, of ample length, that are brightly dyed and
Chiefly worn by Mexican women. Not a
Further Bozo. Not an attempt at cloning.
Shudder to think it.

Bozo, Quid Pro Quo

Names, he knows. Our Bozo can cough up names till
Cows croak. Ask for names in return, however ...
Same-old same-old: "Bundle" (in Old High German),
"Big Mouth" (in Latin).

Bozo Utters a Bon Mot

Asked about increasingly vitriolic
Spats regarding Comedy's tragic center,
Bozo cries, "Ridiculous quibberdicking!
HA ha ha." [Weeping.]

Bozo, Incognito

He's the older guy in the hat. Or wait – the
Tap instructor (cane and corsage) about to
Pay his tab. Or Bartender Joe. Good Jesus!
Everywhere: Bozo.

Song for the Song-maker

"That sorrow passed, and so may this." – "Deor," c. 900 A.D.

Deor is done for,   dashed and defunct.
His tongue's in tatters;   take him away.
Burn his æstel,   bury his books,
And let out a woe: the world is worse.

Hephzibah Cemetery / April 1889

"Tho' always unmarried I have had six children – two are dead – One living southern grandchild, fine boy, who writes to me occasionally." – Walt Whitman, in a letter to John Addington Symonds, August 19, 1890

> Hephzibah means *my delight is in thee,*
> but that light is gone, Walt, that light's been snuffed
> by the rain clouds. The headstones warp open,
> they're plundered by snakes – Zanna half-saves them
> with chalk rubbings. *Why come to Hephzibah?*
> the magnolias moan, with their sickly
> sweet blossoms I taste in my sleep. *Why spread*
> *dumbstruck ashes at the creek's fat mouth?*
> Why do anything, Walt? It's a direct question.
> Zanna sends you love she doesn't have
> to spare and decorates our tent with epitaphs.
> "Dead forever" reads her grandmum's – sadly
> I'm lying. Write me some way to recast
> this sky, rub the clouds to blue slate, wring pulp
> from the sun. Let jackdaws be mourning doves,
> let mourning be delight, let ashes be snow, dust
> sweet enough to eat. Make me take back
> the comment *no love to spare* – Zanna's
> a copperhead angel, a sage-mouthed blossom,
> something to press against in the rain.
>
> Wrecked, moored in Georgia,
>
> Caleb

New Orleans / August 1890

We're selling shaved ice with black kids
by the St. Louis Cathedral. *Scraping by*
is the joke, but Walt if you could see
the spiral stairways by the sugar-mills, taste
the shrimp wind off the riverdocks, touch
the sun on Smoke's fur, if you could spread
out your arms and smell oleander
and orange trees, then, I promise, you'd understand
abundance. Write me back about this city,
tell me who you met: – the organ-grinders
on Bourbon, the nuns by the oven vaults.
Then I'll tell you how Smoke tackles
Jackson Square strays, how Zanna laughs
till tears stream and the black kids point at us.
I'll tell you how ice melts in ninety degrees –
not that much, in a block – but beautifully,
just beautifully, like anything that won't last.

From the lair of the Congo eel,

Caleb

Camden / June 1892

This is the letter no one will see.
This is me in your house, Walt – thirty blocks
from your grave. This is six in the evening,
Mickle Street light, Smoke and Watch raving
like syphilitics in the yard. This is my
heartbreak coda, my withered *Why?*, my stormy
yawp, my deluge off the Delaware.
I can tell you two things: one, Zanna gone
isn't Zanna canceled ... and two, I have
no boots. I've worn them through. You understand
the problem. In a dream, you, Zanna, Smoke,
and I floated over this city. You read
us poems. I've never properly told you
what a great poet I think you are.
Beneath us, men fixed bicycles and drank
steam beer. Women brought the sun up. We watched
this, Walt, in untranslatable wonder.

Packing my bags before the appraisers come,

Caleb

MIKE WHITE

Invitation

To the boy not me
who drowned
in the swollen river
and who returned
for a month of nights
riding my borrowed bike

I say come again come
inside and get warm

now we are older
the river is dry
let us put aside our differences

Tentacled Motherfucker

Lives in the sewers lives on algae lives forever

Steals mail steals checks one child still missing

Sneaks cereal bars from the Nabisco factory dumpster
(when the night guard hears rummaging out back
he puts his earphones on and loudly hums)

Once an uncanny shadow under a bridge
identified by two boys sniffing paint thinner

Makes a moaning sound makes a sobbing sound

Rings the church bell at unlikely hours

Starts weird fires and the sky turns green

Paints ravishing nocturnal murals

In the railroad yard there's a little vegetable garden
no one remembers planting

Wind

Not a remarkable wind.
So when the bistro's patio umbrella
blew suddenly free and pitched
into the middle of the road,
it put a stop to the afternoon.

Something white and amazing
was blocking the way.

A waiter in a clean apron
appeared, not quite
certain, shielding his eyes, wary
of our rumbling engines.

He knelt in the hot road,
making two figures in white, one
leaning over the sprawled,
broken shape of the other,
creaturely, great-winged,
and now so carefully gathered in.

Age of Miracles

Upon a darkening hill
the telescopes turn as one.

They say the stars will fall
by and by, on and on.

LISA WILLIAMS

Gullet

Gnarled vision: a dark fist
rooting among the branches for ripe berries,

like a body of black starlings whose gold beaks
break and split into a clatter of knives

in neighborhood air.
I hear them interrupt the hour.

Wings, spiked feet, and oval bodies
slice through dogwoods' thin, scarred boughs

as they leave and light,
the rose-tipped, drooped, decrepit leaves

shuddering –
The feathers on their backs

spell tapestries of birthing stars,
a cosmos carried.

It is no longer solid, the thing
that would be grabbed and preyed upon,

the thing imagined.
It loses color, becomes

something other than what they saw,
since what they see they take.

Sporadic flare of yellow mouths –
this other fruit

glanced among the color-weeping branches.
They're after berries,

red-orange orbs, persimmon constellations
in the Keatsian nest.

Not spirit, but bulk, pure matter
whose greed disrupts and shatters

whatever's picturesque.
It's divide, land, shake, plumb, pluck

and swallow. A red orb flashes against a yellow
beak, black gap, before the entrance shuts.

I like to watch that part –
take satisfaction in the berry's

roundness as it's caught in pointed lines
before the bird's head tips

to roll it back.
Each berry was a beauty

for some gullet to transform.
They are seekers flying over

fields I know, whose dry, sharp grasses
and weeds puncture the air

under their flight.
They are kin of my tongue, and thievish, and late.

Erratics

> Boulders caught in slow-moving glaciers
> and carried along with the ice.

Around you, this cold mother tongue
trundles without acknowledging
your single presence, dredges chunks
of landscape, troughs great peaks to junk
and sediment, carries you along.

One of the stubborn elements,
one of the ancient wholes gone wrong,
you're just a speck. This pale, cold mother
buries you in her enclosure
of locomotion, her slow lunge

of transparent cavalry. You can't loll
freely inside her, but are rolled
into the stampede of sameness. Dawns
wash blue and violet on her mass
in which frail, muted daylight drowns

through layers of muffling ice. You're pulled
hundreds of miles, for centuries,
trapped in a blank cocoon that cracks
branch slowly in, and re-fuse later.
Her sound is a chorus of fractures. Glass

shatters to veins, black roots. Whole chambers
echo with splintering. When melting
comes it will be the liquid gasp
of adamant impressions loosed
and streaming from you as you catch

on land, too heavy to budge farther.
Headed toward open sea, as ice
will do when its voice becomes less groan,
more supple, that which must abandon,
at last she leaves you: upright and alone.

Snow Covering Leaves of a Magnolia

Perfection stills, admits nothing,
like these white grains cupped and blinding
in lilac light –

What its object "feels,"
if feeling's relevant,
is weight, the burden of surprise,

an iced admonishment
of months coming to fruit
on the vagrant summer's dark green

lustrous skins.
Nostalgia's excess
has been banished.

The new reign's virgin syllables,
in papery increments,
whisper their descent:

This is what you must turn to.
This zeroed sensation.
This blow to sprawl.

Horizons frozen
by a yield of white.
Growth is not virtue.

So the body becomes a statue
in puritan dress.
Nothing to do but stand there

and bear it, revoked,
while perfection lands each earnest
inimical stroke.

CONTRIBUTORS' NOTES AND ACKNOWLEDGMENTS

CRAIG ARNOLD was born in 1967 and educated at Yale University and the University of Utah. He taught poetry at the University of Wyoming, and was the author of two books of poems, *Shells* (1999), and *Made Flesh* (2008). His poems appeared in several anthologies, including *The Best American Poetry 1998* and the *Bread Loaf Anthology of New American Poets,* and in many journals, including *Poetry,* the *Paris Review,* the *New Republic* and the *Yale Review.* He went missing in 2009 while hiking alone on the small Japanese island of Kuchinoerabujima and is presumed to have died from a fall. [Craig Arnold, "Incubus" from *Made Flesh*. Copyright © 2008 by Craig Arnold. Reprinted with the permission of Copper Canyon Press, www.coppercanyonpress.org.]

BRUCE BERGER was a finalist for the Hecht Prize in 2006, 2007 and 2008. His poems have appeared in *Poetry, Barron's,* the *Hudson Review* and other literary journals and anthologies. He Poetry addressing the interpenetrations of life and music has been collected in *Facing the Music.* In 2009 he was sent by the Department of State to represent the United States at a literary conference in northern India, followed by a week of readings in New Delhi and Mumbai. ["Transmigration" first appeared in *Poetry* and "Confession" first appeared in the *Hudson Review*.]

PETER BETHANIS is an Assistant Professor of English at Ball State University in Indiana. He was a finalist for the Hecht Prize in 2005, and his poems and essays have appeared in over fifty literary journals, including *Poetry, Tar River Poetry, Lullwater Review, Haight Ashbury Literary Journal* and *River Review.* He is the co-author of a book, *Dada and Surrealism for Beginners* (Random House, 2007). ["American Future" first appeared in *Poetry*, and "The Deer in the Barns" first appeared in *Aethlon*, and was selected by James Dickey as winner of the Eve of St Agnes Poetry Award, 1995.]

KIMBERLY BURWICK is the author of two collections of poetry: *Has No Kinsmen* (Red Hen Press, 2006) and *Horses in the Cathedral*, winner of the Robert Dana Prize (forthcoming from Anhinga Press, 2011). She was a finalist for the Hecht Prize in 2007, 2008 and

2009. Recently she was awarded the *Black Warrior Review* Poetry Prize and the C.P. Cavafy Prize from the journal *Poetry International*. She teaches for Washington State University.

MICHAELA CARTER was born in Phoenix, Arizona, in 1967 and educated at the University of California at Los Angeles and Warren Wilson College. Nominated for a Pushcart Prize, her poetry has appeared in the *Southern Review*, the *Antioch Review*, *Puerto Del Sol*, *New Letters* and *New England Review,* amongst other journals. She lives in Prescott, Arizona with her two children and teaches creative writing at Yavapai College. ["The Debutante Ball" first appeared in The Chester H. Jones Foundation National Poetry Competition Winners' Anthology, and "When We Speak of Love" first appeared in the *New England Review*.]

KEN CHEN was the 2009 recipient of the Yale Series of Younger Poets Award, the oldest annual literary award in the United States. He was a finalist for the Hecht Prize in 2005. His debut poetry collection *Juvenilia*, was selected by Pulitzer Prize winner Louise Gluck. A graduate of Yale Law School, He is the Executive Director of The Asian American Writers' Workshop (aaww.org), the most prominent literary arts nonprofit in support of Asian American literature. ["My Father and Mother Decide My Future and How Could We Forget Wang Wei?" first appeared in *Palimpsest*.]

SCOTT COFFEL was born in New York City in 1956, and educated at York College. He was a finalist for the Hecht Prize in 2005, 2006 and 2007. His book *Toucans in the Arctic* was published by Etruscan Press and received the Poetry Society of America's 2010 Norma Farber First Book Award. His poems have appeared in *Salmagundi*, *Ploughshares*, *Paris Review*, and elsewhere. He lives in Iowa City, and directs a technical writing program for The University of Iowa. [Scott Coffel, "Light Years from My Redemption," "In the Throes of Advanced Study," "Andrei and Natasha," "Cockeyed Louie," "The Emerald City," "Hordes of Indigent Psychologists," "Mild Worlds Elsewhere" from *Toucans in the Attic*. Copyright © 2010 by Scott Coffel. Reprinted with the permission of The Permissions Company, Inc., on Behalf of Etruscan Press, www.etruscanpress.org.]

ANDREW COX is the author of *The Equation That Explains Everything* (BlazeVOX Books 2010), the chapbook *Fortune Cookies* (*2River View*, 2009) and the hypertext chapbook *Company X* (Wordvirtual, 1999). He lives in University City, MO, the Brooklyn of St. Louis, where he edits *UCity Review* (www.ucityreview.com). ["Two Plus Two Equals Five" and "The American Museum" from *The Equation That Explains Everything*. Copyright © 2010 by Andrew Cox.]

MORRI CREECH is the author of two collections of poetry, the more recent of which, *Field Knowledge*, was awarded the first Hecht Prize in 2005 and was nominated for the *Los Angeles Times* Book Award and the Poet's Prize. He lives in Charlotte, North Carolina, where the teaches at Queens University of Charlotte. ["World Enough," "The Canto of Ulysses," "For the Rebel Angels," "The Resurrection of the Body," "Listening to the Earth" and "Firstfruits" from *Field Knowledge* (The Waywiser Press). Copyright © 2006 by Morri Creech.]

GREGORY CROSBY was a finalist for the Hecht Prize in 2006. He is a former art critic whose poetry has appeared in numerous journals, including *Court Green*, *Copper Nickel* and *Epiphany*, and on a bronze plaque in a park in downtown Las Vegas.

ERICA DAWSON was born in Columbia, MD in 1979 and earned her Ph.D. from the University of Cincinnati. Her first collection, *Big-Eyed Afraid*, was awarded the second Hecht Prize in 2006, and her poems have appeared or are forthcoming in *Best American Poetry 2008, Barrow Street, Literary Imagination, Virginia Quarterly Review*, and other journals and anthologies. She is an Assistant Professor of English and Writing at University of Tampa in Florida. ["Nappyhead," "Doll Baby," "OCD," "Credo," "Parallax" and "Bees in the Attic" from *Big-Eyed Afraid* (The Waywiser Press). Copyright © 2007 by Erica Dawson.]

ANTHONY DEATON is currently the Public Affairs Officer at the U.S. Embassy in Windhoek, Namibia. He was a finalist for the Hecht Prize in 2008 and 2009. He has published a chapbook, *Rhumb Lines* (Sutton Hoo Press), and his work has appeared in the *Gettysburg Review*, *The Nation*, the *Paris Review*, and the *Southeast*

Review, amongst other journals. His past awards include the *Nation*/Discovery Award for poetry, The Campbell Corner Poetry Prize, and an artist grant from the Connecticut Commission of Culture and Tourism. ["After Troy" first appeared in *The Nation*, "The Refusal" first appeared In the *Gettysburg Review* and "Homeward, Angel" first appeared in *Rhumb Lines*.]

MATT DONOVAN was born in Hudson, Ohio in 1973 and received his MFA from New York University. He is the author of *Vellum* (Mariner, 2007), and his poetry and non-fiction have appeared in publications such as *AGNI*, *Kenyon Review*, and *Virginia Quarterly Review*. He chairs the Creative Writing and Literature Department at Santa Fe University of Art and Design. ["Prelude for Musical Glasses" first appeared in *Gettysburg Review* and "Exit Pursued by a Bear" first appeared in *American Poetry Review*."]

MOLLY FISK was born in San Francisco in 1955 and was educated at Harvard. She was a finalist for the Hecht Prize in 2007. Her publications include *The More Difficult Beauty* (Hip Pocket Press, 2010) and *Listening to Winter* (Roundhouse/Heyday Press, 2000). Her poems have been widely published and anthologized. She works as a writing teacher, life coach, and radio commentator in Nevada City, California. ["Prayer for Joe's Taco Lounge, Mill Valley" first appeared in *88: Journal of Contemporary American Poetry*, and "Rowing, November" first appeared in the anthology *Cloud View Poets: Master Classes with David St. John*, and was reprinted on the Radcliffe College Crew's 30th Anniversary webpage.]

MARTHA GREENWALD was born in Red Bank, New Jersey and attended Brandeis University, Iowa State, and was a Wallace Stegner Fellow at Stanford University. Her first collection of poems, *Other Prohibited Items*, was a winner of the 2010 *Mississippi Review* Poetry Prize. Her poems have appeared in such journals as *Slate*, *Poetry*, *MARGIE*, *The Sycamore Review*, and *The Threepenny Review*. She currently resides in Louisville, Kentucky. ["The Last Secretary" first appeared in *Slate* and "Other Prohibited Items" first appeared in *Best New Poets 2008*.]

DANIEL GROVES was a finalist for the Hecht Prize in 2005 and 2006. A graduate of the Writing Seminars at Johns Hopkins University, he now lives in his native Rhode Island. He is the author of *The Lost Boys* (University of Georgia Press/ VQR Poetry Series, 2010), and his poems have appeared in such publications as the *Paris Review,* the *Yale Review,* and *Poetry*. [Daniel Groves, "A Dog's Life," "Portrait," "Novella," and "A Stranger Here" from *The Lost Boys*. Copyright © 2010 by Daniel Groves. Reprinted with the permission of The University of Georgia Press, www.ugapress.org.]

JAMEY HECHT was a finalist for the Hecht Prize in 2006. He is the author of four books: *How to Write About Homer* (2010); *Plato's Symposium: Eros and the Human Predicament* (1999); a translation, *Sophocles' Three Theban Plays: Antigone, Oedipus the Tyrant, Oedipus at Colonus* (2004); and a collection of poems, *Limousine, Midnight Blue: Fifty Frames from the Zapruder Film* (2009). His poetry, criticism and journalism have appeared in *Black Warrior Review, Tikkun, Free Inquiry, Massachusetts Review, E.L.H* and other journals. ["Zapruder Film Frame 155" and "Zapruder Film Frame 197" from *Limousine, Midnight Blue: Fifty Frames from the Zapruder Film*. Copyright © 2009 by Jamey Hecht. Reprinted with the permission of Red Hen Press.]

JAIMEE HILLS was educated at the University of North Carolina at Greensboro and The Johns Hopkins University. Her poems have appeared in *Best New Poets, Blackbird, Poetry Northwest, The 2011 Rhysling Anthology,* and others. She lives and writes in Durham, North Carolina. ["Chlamydia" first appeared in *Waccamaw* and "Nothing Rhymes with Gitmo" first appeared in the *Vocabula Review*.]

KAREN HOLMBERG was a finalist for the Hecht Prize in 2009. Her first book, *The Perseids*, won the Vassar Miller Prize and was published by the University of North Texas Press; her second book, *Axis Mundi*, is the latest winner of the John Ciardi Prize and will be published by BkMk Press in 2012. Individual poems have appeared in such magazines as the *Paris Review, Slate, The Nation, Cimarron Review, Southern Poetry Review, Cave Wall, Nimrod, Subtropics*, and have won her a Discovery/*The Nation* Award. She is an associate professor in Oregon State University's M.F.A. program. ["Imago, *Io Moth*" first appeared in *Cave Wall*, and "Man O' War" first appeared in *Natural Bridge*.]

LESLEY JENIKE was born in Cincinnati, Ohio in 1977. She received her MFA from The Ohio State University in 2003 and her Ph.D. from the University of Cincinnati in 2008. She was a finalist for the Hecht Prize in 2009. Her first book of poems is *Ghost of Fashion* (CW, 2009) and her poems have appeared in the *Gettysburg Review,* the *Southern Review, Poetry, Sou'wester, Gulf Coast,* and other journals. She is currently an assistant professor of English at the Columbus College of Art and Design in Columbus, Ohio. ["Self-Portrait as the Golden Head at the Jardin de Luxembourg" first appeared on diodepoetry.com, and "A Rothko Conversation" first appeared on drunkenboat.com.]

CARRIE JERRELL was born in Petersburg, Indiana in 1976 and was educated at Johns Hopkins University and Texas Tech University. Her first collection, *After the Revival*, was awarded the fourth Hecht Prize in 2008, and her poems have appeared in such publications as *IMAGE*, *Passages North*, *Subtropics*, and *Measure*, among others. She works as an assistant professor and associate director of the low-residency MFA program at Murray State University in Murray, Kentucky. ["The Poet Prays to Her Radio for a Country Song," "The Country-Western Singer's Ex-Wife, Sober in Mendocino County, California," "The Poet Prays to the 9mm under the Driver's Seat," "The Bridesmaid," "The Best Man," "The Maid of Honor," "When the Rider Is Hope," "I Am Thinking of My First Horse," "After the Revival" and "When the Rider is Truth" from *After the Revival* (The Waywiser Press). Copyright © 2009 by Carrie Jerrell.]

ROSE KELLEHER grew up in Massachusetts and lives in Maryland. Her first collection, *Bundle o' Tinder*, was awarded the third Hecht Prize in 2007. Her poems and essays have been published widely, most recently in *New Walk*, *Snakeskin* and the *Raintown Review*. ["Ditty," "Asperger's Muse," "Zeitoun," "Neanderthal Bone Flue," "Impulse," "Noted Sadomasochists," "Lye," "Brockton Man" and "Lovesick" from *Bundle o' Tinder* (The Waywiser Press). Copyright © 2008 by Rose Kelleher.]

DORE KIESSELBACH was raised in California and studied poetry at Oberlin College and the University of Iowa Writers' Workshop. His work has appeared widely in American magazines such as *Antioch Review*, *FIELD* and *New Letters*. He won Britain's Bridport Prize in poetry in 2009. ["The Painted Hall, Lascaux" and "First Hike After Your Mother's Death" first appeared in *Field*.]

ELIZABETH KLISE VON ZERNECK lives in Illinois. She was a finalist for the Hecht Prize in 2008. Her poems have appeared in *Cincinnati Review*, *Crab Orchard Review*, *Measure*, *New York Quarterly*, *Ninth Letter*, *Notre Dame Review*, *The Pinch*, *Potomac Review*, *Rattle*, and *Water-Stone Review*. She has received the Robert Frost Foundation Poetry Award, an International Publication Prize from *Atlanta Review*, and an *Illinois Arts Council* Fellowship Award in Poetry. ["Slant Rhyme," "Illinois Landscape" and "Science and Industry" first appeared in the *Spoon River Poetry Review*.]

ANTHONY LACAVARO was born in Philadelphia, Pennsylvania in 1972 and educated at Hamilton College and the University of Massachusetts at Amherst. His poems have appeared in the *Paris Review*, the *New Republic*, the *Yale Review*, and elsewhere. He works at a bank and serves as a contributing editor for Open City magazine and books, and lives in Brooklyn, New York. ["An Essay on the Body" first appeared in the *Paris Review*, and "Babies" first appeared in *La Petite Zine*.]

MATTHEW LADD was born in Los Angeles and raised in the Texas Panhandle. After completing his undergraduate work in West Texas, he read for the M.Phil. in Divinity at the University of Cambridge. In 2006 he received an M.F.A. in Poetry from the University of Florida. His first collection, *The Book of Emblems*, was awarded the fifth Hecht Prize, in 2009, and his poems have appeared in the *Paris Review, Yale Review, Virginia Quarterly* and *Antioch Review* and elsewhere. He currently lives in New York. ["Envoi," "Imitation," "Poem for K.," "Scenes from a Common Life," "Marcel Proust's Last Summer Holiday," "Klintholm Havn" and "Coelacanth" from *The Book of Emblems* (The Waywiser Press). Copyright © 2010 by Matthew Ladd.]

NICK LANTZ was born in Berkeley, California, and received his MFA from the University of Wisconsin-Madison. He was a finalist for the Hecht Prize in 2007. His recent books include *We Don't Know We Don't Know* and *The Lightning That Strikes the Neighbors' House*. His poems have appeared in *Southern Review, FIELD,* and *Gulf Coast,* among others. He teaches creative writing and lives in Lancaster, Pennsylvania. ["The Year We Blew Up the Whale – Florence, Oregon" and "Challenger": Lantz, Nick. *The Lightning that Strikes the Neighbours' House.* © 2010 by the Board Regents of the University of Wisconsin System. Reprinted courtesy of The University of Wisconsin Press.]

JULIE LARIOS was born in Ellensburg, Washington, in 1949. She received her MFA from the University of Washington. Her poems have appeared in *The Atlantic*, *Ploughshares*, the *Threepenny Review*, *Field*, *Margie* and other magazines, as well as the *Best American Poetry* series. Her libretto for a penny opera titled *All Three Acts of a Sad Play Performed Entirely in Bed* was recently chosen for the VOX series of the New York City Opera. She teaches at The Vermont College of Fine Arts and lives in Seattle. ["Woman with the Beak of an Octopus" first appeared in the *Indiana Review*.]

DENNIS LONEY lives in Washington, D.C. with his wife and daughters and is the Director of Digital Products for *The New Republic*. He was a finalist for the Hecht Prize in 2005. His poetry has appeared in *32 Poems, Able Muse, The Flea, Measure, Sewanee Theological Review, Shit Creek Review, Sugar House Review*, and elsewhere. ["The Man Under the Dump" first appeared in the *Sewanee Theological Review*.]

DORA MALECH was a finalist for the Hecht Prize In 2007 and 2008. She is the author of *Shore Ordered Ocean* (Waywiser, 2009) and *Say So* (Cleveland State University Poetry Center, 2011). Her poems have appeared in the *New Yorker*, *Poetry*, and *Poetry London*, among other journals. She earned a B.A. from Yale and an M.F.A. from the Iowa Writers' Workshop. A 2010 Ruth Lilly Poetry Fellow, she lives in Iowa City, Iowa. ["Let Me Explain," "Makeup," "Delivery Rhyme," "Here Name Your," "Push, Pull," "Drought Year," "Dreaming in New Zealand" and "A Shortcut" from *Shore Ordered*

Ocean (The Waywiser Press). Copyright © 2009 by Dora Malech.]

CHRISTOPHER TODD MATTHEWS was born in California and educated at Kalamazoo College, Warren Wilson College (MFA), and the University of Michigan (Ph.D.). His poems have appeared in the *Antioch Review*, *Beloit Poetry Journal*, *FIELD*, the *Gettysburg Review*, *Indiana Review*, *Shenandoah*, and elsewhere. He currently teaches at Washington and Lee University in Lexington, Virginia. ["The Red Balloon" first appeared in *West Branch*, and "The Roman Baths in June" first appeared in *Shenandoah*.]

NICOLE MELANSON grew up in Boston, studied at New York University and Oxford, and now lives in Sydney with her husband and their four young sons. She writes both poetry and fiction, has been published in numerous literary journals, and was recently awarded a grant from the Australia Council for the Arts. She is currently working on a novel.

DEREK MONG was born in Portland, Oregon in 1981, grew up in Ohio, and received degrees from Denison University and the University of Michigan. He was a finalist for the Hecht Prize in 2008. He is the author of the poetry collection *Other Romes* (Saturnalia Books, 2011), and his work has appeared in the *Missouri Review*, the *Kenyon Review*, the *Southern Review*, and elsewhere. He lives in San Francisco. ["Equivalents," "Vitruvian Man," "O h i o –," "Mia," "Fellini's Satyricon" and "Period" from *Other Romes*. Copyright © 2011 by Derek Mong. Reprinted with the permission of Saturnalia Books. "Equivalents" first appeared in the *Kenyon Review*, "Vitruvian Man" first appeared in the *Missouri Review*, "O h i o –" first appeared in *Alehouse*, "Mia" first appeared In *TriQuarterly* and "Period" first appeared in the *Michigan Quarterly Review*.]

SIERRA NELSON was born in Berkeley, California and educated at Vassar College and University of Washington. Her collaborative chapbooks include *TYPO*, *Desire & Flotation Devices*, and *Who Are We; I Take Back the Sponge Cake* with visual artist Loren Erdrich is forthcoming from Rose Metal Press. Nelson's poems have appeared in *Poetry Northwest*, *Crazyhorse*, and *DIAGRAM*, among other magazines. She works as a teacher and lives in Seattle. ["We'll Always Have Carthage" first appeared in *Poetry Northwest*.]

MICHAEL LEE PHILLIPS was born in Trona, California, and received a BA from Fresno State. He was a finalist for the Hecht Prize in 2008. His poems have appeared in *The Antioch Review, Beloit Poetry Journal, Cimarron Review, The Literary Review, New York Quarterly, The Stinging Fly* (Ireland), and *Pearl*. His book, *Nights of Naked Mannequins,* was published in 2010 by Austin Hall Press. He resides in Ridgecrest, California. ["The Man in the Barrel" first appeared in *Nimrod* and "Shooting at Lamar" first appeared in *Potomac Review*.]

JESSICA PIAZZA was born in Brooklyn, has a B.S. in Journalism from Boston University, an M.A. in English and Creative Writing from the University of Texas at Austin and is currently a Ph.D. candidate in English Literature and Creative Writing at the University of Southern California. She is a co-founder of *Bat City Review,* an editor at *Gold Line Press,* a contributing editor at *The Offending Adam* and has blogged for *The Best American Poetry* and *Barrelhouse*. Her poems have appeared or are forthcoming in *The Missouri Review, 32 Poems, The National Poetry Review, Agni, Indiana Review, Mid-American Review, Rattle, No Tell Motel, 42 Opus* and *Forklift, Ohio*. ["Kopohobia" first appeared in the *National Poetry Review*, and "Melophobia" first appeared in *If Magazine*.]

AARON POOCHIGIAN lived in Greece on fellowship from 2003 until 2004 and earned his Ph.d. in Classics from the University of Minnesota in 2006. His translations of Greek poetry include: *Stung With Love: The Poems of Sappho* (Penguin 2009) and *Aratus: Phaenomena* (Johns Hopkins 2010), and two forthcoming volumes: *Aeschylus: Persians, Seven against Thebes and Suppliants* (Johns Hopkins 2011) and Apollonius' *Adventures of the Argonauts* (Penguin 2012). He was awarded a 2010-11 NEA Grant in Translation, and his poems and translations have appeared in such journals as the *Financial Times, Poems Out Loud* and *Poetry Magazine*. ["The Marriage of Peleus and Thetis" first appeared in *Arion: A Journal of the Arts and Humanities*.]

ALISON POWELL was a finalist for the Hecht Prize In 2007. Her poetry has appeared in *AGNI*, *Crazyhorse*, *Black Warrior Review*, *Denver Quarterly*, *Caketrain*, and other journals, and in the anthology *Best New Poets 2006*; she has work forthcoming in the *Boston Review*. She is currently pursuing a Ph.D. in English Literature at the City University of New York Graduate Center, and she teaches at Hunter College. ["Shangri-la" first appeared in *Black Warrior Review*," "Decorum" first appeared in *Guernica*, "Edema" first appeared in *Best New Poets 2006*, and "The Raw Fields" first appeared in *Runes: A Review of Poetry*.]

CHRIS PREDDLE was a finalist for the Hecht Prize In 2005, 2006 and 2008. He was born in London in 1943 and educated at Stonyhurst College in Lancashire, where he was taught by Peter Levi. He worked in British public libraries and as a librarian for two child care charities. He has retired to the village of Holme on a shoulder of the Pennines in West Yorkshire, where he lives with his wife Jacqui. His second collection is *Cattle Console Him* (Waywiser, 2010). His first was *Bonobos* (Biscuit Publishing, 2001). ["Water Sonnets," "Not Catullus," "The Arrowloop," "Earthmover," "Ruin," "First Letter to Ed," "Cattle Console Him" and "Groundsel" from *Cattle Console Him* (The Waywiser Press). Copyright © 2010 by Chris Preddle.]

BOBBY C. ROGERS grew up in West Tennessee and was educated at Union University, the University of Tennessee at Knoxville, and the University of Virginia. He was a finalist for the Hecht Prize in 2008. His book *Paper Anniversary* won the 2009 Agnes Lynch Starrett Poetry Prize at University of Pittsburgh Press. He is Professor of English and Writer-in-Residence at Union University in Jackson, Tennessee. He lives in Memphis with his wife and son and daughter. ["Burning the Walls," "Nocturne," "Pastoral," and "Newground" from *Paper Anniversary*, by Bobby C. Rogers, © 2010. Reprinted with permission of the University of Pittsburgh Press.]

JOHN SUROWIECKI was born in Meriden, Connecticut, in 1943, and was educated at the University of Connecticut. He was a finalist for the Hecht Prize in 2005. He is the author of three books of poetry and five chapbooks. A new book, *Mr. Z., Mrs. Z., J.Z., S.Z.,* is scheduled for publication by Ugly Duckling Press. He also received the Poetry Foundation Pegasus Award for verse drama and the Pablo Neruda Prize. Poems of his have recently appeared in *Alaska Quarterly Review, Folio, Colere* and *Mississippi Review.* He lives in Amston, Connecticut. ["The Hat City after the Men Stopped Wearing Hats," "Connecticut Invaded by Chinese Communists (1951)," "The Childless Couple's Child," "Americanization of a Poem by Wislawa Szymborska" and "The Wisest Aunt, Telling the Saddest Tales" from *The Hat City after the Men Stopped Wearing Hats*, by John Surowiecki, © 2007. Reprinted with permission of The Word Works Press, Washington DC. ["The Hat City after the Men Stopped Wearing Hats" first appeared in *Poetry*, "The Childless Couple's Child" first appeared in *Chachalaca Poetry Review*, and "The Wisest Aunt, Telling the Saddest Tales" first appeared in *Caduceus*.]

MICHAEL SWAN was born in London in 1936, and studied modern languages at Oxford University. He was a finalist for the Hecht Prize in 2009. He has published two poetry collections: *When They Come For You* (Frogmore Press) and *The Shapes Of Things* (Oversteps Books). His poems have also appeared in numerous magazines. He works as a freelance writer of English language teaching and reference materials, and lives in Oxfordshire. ["Not What I Meant," "How Everything Is" and "Lance-Corporal Swan" from Michael Swan, *The Shapes of Things*, © 2011. Reprinted with permission of Oversteps Press.]

BRADFORD GRAY TELFORD was born in El Paso, raised in Dallas, and educated at Princeton, Columbia, and the University of Houston. He was a finalist for the Hecht Prize In 2005, 2006 and 2007. His first collection of poems, *Perfect Hurt,* was published by Waywiser in 2008, and his work has appeared in *Ploughshares*, *Yale Review, Southwest Review,* and *BOMB*. He teaches high school English and lives in Houston. ["At the Theatre," "The Woman Who Was Not Matisse," *"The Conversation,"* "The Backsplash," "Portrait of the Artist's Mother at the Analyst," *"Melia azederach,"* "September" and *"For Further Information"* from *Perfect Hurt* (The Waywiser Press). Copyright © 2009 by Bradford Gray Telford.]

JAMIE JOEL THOMAS was born in Detroit in 1973 and was educated at Western Michigan University and the University of Houston. His first book, *Etch and Blur*, is due out in the fall of 2011, and his work has appeared in *32 Poems, The Missouri Review, Rattle, Verse and on Verse Daily*. He is currently a Visiting Professor in the Languages and Literature Department at Ferris State University. [Towing Water to Australia" first appeared in *RHINO*, and "Youth Longs to Live" first appeared in *Verse*.]

MATTHEW THORBURN was a finalist for the Hecht Prize in 2007 and 2009. He is the author of *Subject to Change* and has two forthcoming books of poems, *Every Possible Blue* (CW Books, 2012) and *This Time Tomorrow* (Waywiser, 2013). His poems have also appeared in the *Paris Review, Poetry Northwest* and *Ploughshares*. He lives in New York City, where he works on the business staff of an international law firm. "Now is Always a Good Time" first appeared in the *Paris Review*, "Horse Poetica" first appeared in *Passages North*, "Gravy Boat," "Woken Each Morning by the Glad Laughter of Birds" and "Self-Portrait with Unmentionables" first appeared in *Pool*," "Horn of Plenty" first appeared in *RealPoetik* and "Still Life" (originally entitled "Every Possible Blue" first appeared in *Diode*.]

D. H. TRACY works at a technology company in Champaign, Illinois.' His book of poems, *Janet's Cottage*, is the winner of the 2011 *New Criterion* Poetry Prize and is forthcoming from St. Augustine's Press.["The Explorer at Eureka Dunes" first appeared in *Poetry*, and "AWOL" first appeared in the *Yale Review*.]

BARBARA LOUISE UNGAR was born in Worcester, Massachusetts in 1956 and was educated at Stanford University and the City University of New York. Her published collections of poetry are *Thrift, The Origin of the Milky Way* (which won the Gival Poetry Prize and three other awards), *Charlotte Brontë, You Ruined My Life*, and several chapbooks. Her poems have been published in *Salmagundi*, the *Minnesota Review*, the *Cream City Review*, the *Literary Review*, and many others. An English professor at The College of Saint Rose in Albany, she lives in Saratoga Springs, New York. ["Embryology," "Riddle" and "Matryoshka" from *The Origin of the Milky Way*. Copyright © 2007 by Barbara Louise Ungar. Reprinted with the permission of The Gival Press.]

CODY WALKER was born in Baltimore, Maryland, in 1967, and educated at the University of Wisconsin, the University of Arkansas, and the University of Washington. He was a finalist for the Hecht Prize in 2005 and 2006. His first poetry collection, *Shuffle and Breakdown*, was published by Waywiser in 2008. His work appears in *Parnassus*, *Slate*, and *The Best American Poetry*. He teaches English at the University of Michigan and lives in Ann Arbor. ["Update," "The Cheney Correspondence (Selected)," "All Poetry is Political," "Earlier Today, Archival Edition," "Offenders," "'The Mould of a Dog-Corpse'," "Bozo Sapphics," "Song for the Song-Maker," "Hephzibah Cemetery / April 1889," "New Orleans / August 1890," "Camden / June 1892" from *Shuffle and Breakdown*, by Cody Walker, © 2008.]

MIKE WHITE hails originally from Montreal and now lives in Salt Lake City. He earned a doctoral degree in Literature and Creative Writing from the University of Utah. He was a finalist for the Hecht Prize in 2009. His first book of poetry is *How to Make a Bird with Two Hands* (The Word Works, 2012). His poems have appeared in *Poetry*, the *New Republic*, and the *Threepenny Review*. ["Invitation" and "Wind" first appeared in *West Branch*, "Tentacled Motherfucker" first appeared in *Pleiades*, "Uncommonly Old Couple Humping" first appeared in *RUNES* and "Age of Miracles" first appeared in the *Connecticut Review*.]

LISA WILLIAMS was born in Nashville in 1966 and was educated at Belmont University, the University of Cincinnati, and the University of Virginia. She was a finalist for the Hecht Prize in 2005 and 2006. Her previous publications include *The Hammered Dulcimer* and *Woman Reading to the Sea*, and her poems appear in the *Cincinnati Review*, *Shenandoah*, *Southwest Review*, and other magazines. She teaches at Centre College in Danville, Kentucky. ["Snow Covering Leaves of a Magnolia," "Erratics," "Gullet," from *Woman Reading to the Sea* by Lisa Williams. Copyright © 2008 by Lisa Williams. Used by permission of W.W. Norton & Company, Inc. "Snow Falling on Leaves of a Magnolia" first appeared in *Salmagundi* and "Gullet" first appeared in the *Southern Review*.]

A Note About Joseph Harrison

Joseph Harrison was born in Richmond, Virginia, grew up in Virginia and Alabama, and studied at Yale and Johns Hopkins Universities. His books of poetry are *Someone Else's Name* (Waywiser, 2003), which was chosen as one of five poetry books of the year for 2004 by the *Washington Post*, and *Identity Theft* (Waywiser, 2008). His poems have appeared in such anthologies as *The Best American Poetry 1998*, *180 More Extraordinary Poems for Every Day*, The Library of America's *American Religious Poems*, the Penguin Pocket *Anthology of Poetry*, the Penguin Pocket *Anthology of Literature*, and *The Swallow Anthology of New American Poets*, and in many journals. In 2005 he received an Academy Award in Literature from the American Academy of Arts and Letters; in 2008 he was awarded a Guggenheim Fellowship in Poetry. He is also the editor, with Damiano Abeni, and wrote the introduction to *Un mondo che non può essere migliore* (Luca Sossella, 2008), a bilingual selection of John Ashbery's poetry which won a Special Prize from the Premio Napoli. Since 2008 he has been the Senior American Editor for Waywiser. He lives in Baltimore.

Other Books from Waywiser

Poetry

Al Alvarez, *New & Selected Poems*
George Bradley, *A Few of Her Secrets*
Robert Conquest, *Penultimata*
Morri Creech, *Field Knowledge*
Peter Dale, *One Another*
Erica Dawson, *Big-Eyed Afraid*
B. H. Fairchild, *The Art of the Lathe*
Jeffrey Harrison, *The Names of Things: New & Selected Poems*
Joseph Harrison, *Identity Theft*
Joseph Harrison, *Someone Else's Name*
Anthony Hecht, *Collected Later Poems*
Anthony Hecht, *The Darkness and the Light*
Carrie Jerrell, *After the Revival*
Rose Kelleher, *Bundle o' Tinder*
Mark Kraushaar, *The Uncertainty Principle*
Matthew Ladd, *The Book of Emblems*
Dora Malech, *Shore Ordered Ocean*
Eric McHenry, *Potscrubber Lullabies*
Eric McHenry & Nicholas Garland: *Mommy Daddy Evan Sage*
Timothy Murphy, *Very Far North*
Ian Parks, *Shell Island*
Chris Preddle: *Cattle Console Him*
Christopher Ricks, ed. *Joining Music with Reason:*
34 Poets, British and American, Oxford 2004-2009
Daniel Rifenburgh, *Advent*
W. D. Snodgrass: *Not for Specialists: New & Selected Poems*
Mark Strand, *Blizzard of One*
Bradford Gray Telford, *Perfect Hurt*
Cody Walker, *Shuffle and Breakdown*
Deborah Warren, *The Size of Happiness*
Clive Watkins, *Jigsaw*
Richard Wilbur, *Anterooms*
Richard Wilbur, *Mayflies*
Richard Wilbur, *Collected Poems 1943-2004*
Norman Williams, *One Unblinking Eye*
Greg Williamson, *A Most Marvelous Piece of Luck*

OTHER BOOKS FROM WAYWISER

FICTION

Gregory Heath, *The Entire Animal*
Matthew Yorke, *Chancing It*

ILLUSTRATED

Nicholas Garland, *I wish ...*
Eric McHenry & Nicholas Garland: *Mommy Daddy Evan Sage*

NON-FICTION

Neil Berry, *Articles of Faith: The Story of British Intellectual Journalism*
Mark Ford, *A Driftwood Altar: Essays and Reviews*
Richard Wollheim, *Germs: A Memoir of Childhood*